How to Sew, Use, and Clean Cloth Diapers

with tutorials for Cloth wipes, unpaper towels, & more!

2ND Edition

Danielle Pientka

Copyright © 2017 by Danielle Pientka

All rights reserved.

Cover photo Copyright © 2017 by Jody McKinley Photography

All rights reserved

1st Edition published under the title "The complete guide to Using, laundering, and Sewing Reusable cloth"

CONTENTS

Introduction 6

1 Why Make the Switch to Cloth Products? 7

2 How to Care for Reusable Cloth Products 16
    Prepping Cloth Diapers 16
    Wash Routines 16
    Stripping 23
    Getting Rid of Stains 23
    Washing Reusable Products Without Electricity 24
    Special Warnings 25

3 Types of Reusable Cloth products 27
    Cloth Diapers 27
    Cloth Wipes and Family Cloth 31
    Nursing Pads 32
    Unpaper Towels 33
    Handkerchiefs 34
    Napkins 35
    Menstrual Pads (Mama Cloth) 36
    Cloth Swim Diapers 38
    Wet Bags 39
    Refrigerator Liners 41
    Reusable Snack Bags 42
    Fabric Gift Bags 43

4 Storage Solutions for Reusable Cloth 44
Cloth Diapers 44
Cloth Wipes, Cloth Napkins, and Handkerchiefs 45
Unpaper Towels 45
Wet Bags 47
Mama Cloth or Cloth Menstrual Pads 48

5 Preparing to Sew Cloth Diapers 49
Choosing a Pattern 49
Choosing Your Supplies 50
Calculating Your Supplies 57
How to Make a Wood Pattern Form 61
Sewing an Entire Stash Fast 63
Time Commitment for Sewing Diapers Assembly-Line Style 66

6 How to Sew Cloth Diapers 68
How to Sew a Cloth Diaper With Pockets 68
How to Sew a Cloth Diaper Cover 80
How to Sew a Cloth Diaper Insert 85
Adding Custom Touches to Cloth Diapers: Ruffles and More 91
Options for Sewing Cloth Diapers on a Budget 99
Common Mistakes When Sewing Cloth Diapers 103
Repairing Cloth Diapers 105
Upgrades for Used Diapers 106
Selling Used Cloth Diapers 109

7 Sewing Other Reusable Cloth products 111
How to Sew Cloth Wipes, Family Cloth, Unpaper Towels, & Cloth Napkins 111
How to Sew Nursing Pads 113
How to Sew Handkerchiefs 115
How to Sew Menstrual Pads (Mama Cloth) 116
How to Sew Wet Bags 123
How to Sew Refrigerator Liners 129
How to Sew Reusable Snack Bags 130
How to Sew Fabric Gift Bags 135

8 Make Your Own Cloth-Diaper-Friendly Diaper Rash Spray 142

Conclusion 144

Links for Further Research 146

INTRODUCTION

My name is Danielle, and I'm a cloth addict. When I was pregnant with my first son, my friend introduced me to the idea of cloth diapering. We were shopping around at a local consignment store—I had a chance to touch a cloth diaper, and I was hooked. They are so soft, and I couldn't imagine anything more comfortable for my baby.

I started cloth diapering and using cloth wipes when my first son was born over four years ago. Now I've switched over to cloth items for the majority of our daily needs. Not only do I use cloth, I also sew most of our cloth products. Most of them are fairly straightforward to sew, too. I write a lot about reusable products and how to sew them on my blog, www.diydanielle.com.

I'm attracted to reusable cloth products for many reasons that go beyond just being ecofriendly. This book explores the many benefits to reusable cloth products, so even if you aren't ready to jump on the tree-hugging wagon, I'm hoping I can help you make the switch for other reasons.

Thanks for taking the time to read this book.

Disclosure: I am not a medical professional. I am a mom, and I formed the opinions in this book through my own research and experience.

1 Why Make the Switch to Cloth Products?

When I was first introduced to reusable cloth products, it was easy for me to get caught up in the "gross" factor—would it be sanitary, and could I keep my reusable products clean and looking nice? Would this be too much work? Would they be easy to use? Would my husband absolutely refuse to use the cloth diapers on my son? How would I combat naysayers who say that I wouldn't keep it up or that making the switch was a terrible idea?

To combat these fears and stay committed to reusable cloth products, I focused on the many benefits of using cloth. I'm going to discuss a few of these in depth.

It's pretty.

This was a major selling point for me; I love being able to customize my reusable items using attractive fabrics. When I sew something beautiful, I love showing it off. If you know someone who cloth diapers, chances are you've seen their kids running around in just a diaper when it's nice out. That's because we love cloth diapers more than we love clothing.

People get creative with cloth diapers, too. I've seen or made cloth diapers with ruffles, tails, and a myriad of fabrics. Some people will even make cloth diapers using interior fabric for their least favorite football team—as in, "poop on the Ravens." (No offense to Ravens fans. I know absolutely nothing about football, so I just picked our local team for an example.) Likewise, plenty of others might use interior fabric for their favorite team because that's an area of the diaper you will see a lot of while changing your baby. And who doesn't love to look at their favorite fabric?

As cloth products have become more popular, I've seen an increase in the variety of fabric options available to make your own products. PUL (short for polyurethane laminate) is usually the waterproof fabric of choice for cloth diapers, and there are now many pattern and color choices available. I also use PUL for reusable nursing and menstrual pads. In addition to PUL, cloth products often incorporate flannel because it is absorbent and is generally available in a variety of patterns at your local craft store.

It's economical.

Using cloth saves money. It's hard to really know how much because the amount saved depends on the item, the person using the item, and how long the item is used, among other factors. We still have disposable products in our home for guests and for us to use when the wet bags (used for storing dirty cloth products) are all in the wash, but our overall use of paper products such as paper towels and toilet paper has decreased substantially.

Cloth diapers specifically have saved our family a lot of money. When I first started cloth diapering, I purchased diapers from major brand names at around $20 each. I was able to save money when I bought them by looking for deals such as "buy five, get one free." I also ordered some from China for $5 each. We used those for the first six months of my oldest son's life until I sewed a stash of cloth diapers large enough to justify selling the diapers I'd originally purchased. I sold the $5 diapers for $4 each and the $20 diapers for $10–15 each. I had a lot of interest when I advertised them on Craigslist, and I felt like I made most of my money back.

The original diapers I made cost about $6–10 each to sew, and we used them for four years with our two older sons. I sold most of them without the inserts for $5 each. I discounted or gave away a few diapers that had damage or needed repairs. Usually the first thing that will need replaced on a cloth diaper is the elastic or the hook and loop (commonly referred to as Velcro), both of which can be easily replaced to extend a diaper's life.

At first, I made mostly pocket diapers, which are more expensive to buy or sew. Your savings will be much greater if you use other types of cloth diapers such as covers with prefolds. We believe that pocket diapers are more convenient, so that was what we opted for. (Note: If you're unfamiliar with cloth diaper terminology like "pockets" or "prefolds," don't worry. Chapter 3 will tell you everything you need to know.)

No chemicals.

I try to remain conscious of how certain chemicals might affect my family while still trying to balance the overabundance of information available to us these days. It's a fine line that I think many parents walk.

If you use cloth products, you won't have the same exposure to the chemicals that are in disposable products, especially diapers, which can irritate certain babies' skin. I have also heard women claim that the chemicals in some disposable feminine products can cause menstrual cramping and extended periods, and that switching to cloth menstrual pads helped to decrease such symptoms dramatically.

Are disposable products going to hurt you or your child? Maybe not. This is a major topic of debate, and it's hard to sort through the information to get the facts. Given the other benefits to cloth, it made sense for my family to switch, but I still use some disposable products when I need to make life easier and decrease my stress level. I err on the side of decreasing chemical exposure rather than removing it completely.

It can cause fewer rashes.

This applies more to cloth diapers, nursing pads, and menstrual pads than other reusable products, but I generally find that a soft fabric handkerchief is gentler than a paper tissue on my nose when I'm sick. If my nose is particularly sensitive, I can even wet the fabric to make it even gentler. This means less redness, too, which is great.

Those with more sensitive skin may be able to avoid rashes by not using disposable products that may contain plastics. I struggled with disposable nursing pads and menstrual pads until I switched to cloth. I would have never realized that the plastic-based ingredients were an issue for me if I hadn't switched to reusable cloth products. It was just something I dealt with every month.

One of the major reasons that many parents switch to cloth diapers is that their baby reacts to disposables. Although some people do still struggle with rashes when cloth diapering, there are two potential causes that have easy solutions. First, you must figure out a good washing routine. If your diaper isn't getting completely clean, residual ammonia can cause rashes. Stripping (more on that later) the diapers and then finding a wash routine that works for you can solve this issue. Second, you must be mindful of the fabric used in your diapers. For example, microfiber inserts can cause rashes if they are directly against the skin. Some kids also may have trouble with certain fabrics or detergents, so you need to rule out allergies.

If you can find a routine that works for you, you'll probably be able to avoid some skin issues that might be problematic with disposable items.

It's better for the environment.

Cloth products don't contribute to build up in landfills the same way that disposable products do. Eventually they will need to be thrown out, but many cloth products can be composted or even recycled. The same cannot be said of most disposable diapers or menstrual pads.

Paper napkins, toilet paper, and paper towels can be composted, but most people probably don't take this extra step. And with toilet paper, composting isn't a good option because you don't want to add harmful bacteria from human or animal feces into your food garden.

It is cleaner.

This is where some of you may disagree with me, and I understand. When I first started using reusable products, I also worried about cleanliness. However, as I've gotten used to using cloth over the years, I haven't noticed a lack of cleanliness—I've actually noticed some improvements.

Disposable toilet paper leaves residue. A wet cloth wipe cleans all of your areas like a wash cloth would and leaves you clean and paper-free. Cloth wipes are awesome for potty training for this reason. I find it really difficult to wipe my oldest son with toilet paper after he uses the toilet—and I don't want to use disposable wipes because they can clog the sewer systems and have the potential to cause plumbing problems. Nothing is easier to wipe with than a wet cloth.

For cloth diapers, it's really a game changer for cleanliness. A month after my first son was born, I was at a doctor's appointment with him. I had him in a disposable diaper because I was using up the last of the stash we'd gotten from the hospital. He had a major explosion—I was in the bathroom with him, and there was poop everywhere. It was all the way up to his neck. I had a dirty diaper to dispose of, an entire baby to clean, and a grossly dirty outfit. Fortunately, I had cloth wipes on me. I was able to wet them in the sink, give him a "bath" on the changing table by wiping him up thoroughly with the wipes, and put both the dirty wipes and the dirty outfit into a wet bag. The wet bag, when zippered, contained both the smell and the grossness until we got home and I could wash it all. A few cloth wipes can do the job of an entire package of disposable wipes because they're thicker. You can also use hot water to wet them, which makes the experience of getting cleaned more pleasant for your child. I was so thankful to have them on me.

I discovered that day that disposable diapers absolutely do not contain waste like cloth diapers do. This is a matter of how the diapers are made. If you lay a cloth diaper and a disposable diaper side by side, you'll notice that they have some structural differences. Cloth diapers have many different options in terms of how you can make them so you can create a diaper that works well for your child—for example, you can add gussets if your child has issues with explosions (although I've never had trouble with cloth diapers unless my child had a terrible stomach bug).

Overall, cloth diapers consist of a few different features that make them fit better than disposables:

1. Most cloth diapers have elastic along the back of the diaper so it fits snuggly around the baby's waist. This prevents waste from exploding up and out of the back of the diaper.
2. The elastic along the legs fits a little snugger, and some cloth diapers allow you to adjust the leg elastic to fit your child better.
3. Most one-size-fits-all cloth diapers are adjustable in several different ways, which allows you to get just the right fit for your child. You can adjust the waist of the diaper so it's snug, and most have a way to snap the diapers down to adjust how far up the diaper comes on your child's stomach.
4. If you sew cloth diapers, you have the ability to create a pattern that works perfectly to fit your child. Disposable diapers are designed to fit the most kids possible in a particular size range.

It's fun to sew or shop for reusable products.

I don't know if I need to mention this, but it's FUN to create awesome diapers or other reusable products. There are so many pretty fabrics. I also personally enjoy having pretty fabrics to use during my menstrual cycle…periods are so bleh and it's nice to have something enjoyable about that time. It's not much, but it's something to look forward to!

If you don't sew, it's fun to shop for reusable diapers. There are some custom diapers that sell for $200 or more in auctions because they're just that awesome. If you're in the market, it's worth checking out HyenaCart and Etsy to see what's available. A quality cloth diaper will usually start around $18–30. When you start getting into truly customized diapers, you may pay $50 or more.

2 How to Care for Reusable Cloth Products

Prepping Cloth Diapers

Some types of cloth diapers need to be prepped before their first use. In the past, experts have said to boil or wash them repeatedly to prep them. I've found that one wash is usually sufficient, and recent research seems to suggest that this is the new recommendation. Some types of fabric do gain absorbency with more washes, however. This is particularly true for prefolds and inserts.

If you purchase used cloth diapers, you must bleach your diapers to avoid the spread of bacteria. (For more detailed information, see FluffLove University's article on Bleaching Cloth Diapers.)

Wash Routines

Washing cloth diapers and other cloth products always seems to be what turns people off to reusable products, but it's really not difficult or gross if you do it right. Yes, you have to rinse the solid waste off in the toilet, but if you're changing a diaper then you're handling poop regardless of what kind of diaper you use, and hopefully you are also washing your hands very well afterward.

HOW TO SEW, USE, AND CLEAN CLOTH DIAPERS

Wet bag hanging in our bathroom.

Rinsing

Always rinse solid waste before putting diapers in the washing machine unless your baby is exclusively breastfed. Waste from breastfed babies will dissolve in water, so you can just run those diapers through the wash.

Once you introduce solid foods, you'll need to rinse solid waste off in the toilet before machine washing. Some people choose to use a diaper sprayer and a splash guard for this, but I find it's faster to do it the old-fashioned way. First, I remove the insert from the pocket diaper and put the insert into a wet bag. Then I take the pocket diaper shell and swish it (dirty side down) in the toilet water. If the waste is solid, you really don't need to do all of that—you can just dump it into the toilet.

If you opt for a sprayer, there are SprayPal buckets available to purchase that prevent water from going everywhere when you spray your diaper down. A similar bucket would be fairly easy to DIY if you feel inspired; they're essentially a bucket with a clip. I tried to make one for myself but felt that there was just too much going on—rinsing in the toilet felt faster. When I had only one kid, I was much keener on having a bunch of baby equipment. By the time the second baby came along, I just wanted to get things done as fast and with as little extra stuff as possible.

Alternatively, some people use disposable liners for cloth diapers. You lay the liner on top of the cloth diaper between your child's bottom and the diaper. When you change the diaper, just remove the liner and flush it down the toilet with any solid waste. Liners work well, but they add to the expense of cloth diapering, so I prefer not to use them. However, I would use them in a heartbeat if I knew my child was on a pretty consistent pooping schedule and I could just use one or two a day.

This is my cloth diaper routine once we introduce solids: diapers with only liquid waste go directly into a wet bag in the bathroom. For solid waste diapers, I use the process described above. Then I make sure to squeeze out any extra water and put the shell into the wet bag until I have a full load of diapers to wash.

Similar to cloth diapers, don't put anything in the washer with your cloth products that won't dissolve. For example, if you use cloth napkins or unpaper towels, make sure that large food scraps don't go into the washing machine.

Washing and Drying

Learning how to wash my cloth diapers has actually taught me a lot about washing machines and laundry in general. I've learned quite a bit about detergents and how they work, too. It's interesting, but you really just need to work out a good routine and stick to it. I have my wash routine framed on the laundry room wall so that if anyone else decides to help out, they won't do something disastrous like add fabric softener (more on that later).

Dryer full of clean cloth products.

I wash my cloth diapers, diaper inserts, cloth wipes, wet bags, and menstrual pads together. Kitchen items like unpaper towels usually end up in a load with bath towels.

When you wash your cloth products, you'll need to be aware of what type of fabric they're made of. Some people use wool covers for their cloth diapers; I won't address how to clean those because we don't use wool, and I don't want to give you incorrect information. Flannel fabric, which is commonly used for unpaper towels or cloth wipes, will be fine with a hot wash and dry cycle.

PUL fabric—the most common fabric for cloth diapers—was originally made as a waterproof material to use in hospitals. It's made to withstand very hot washing and drying cycles for sanitation reasons. I've noticed, however, that some cloth diaper manufacturers state to not use hot water or hot dry cycles; this is due to delamination, which can occur when the laminate layer separates from the fabric on the PUL, essentially rendering your diapers useless because they aren't waterproof without the laminate layer. That said, I've been cloth diapering for over four years and have never had an issue. Buying quality PUL is important.

When I sew PUL, I don't need to prewash for shrinkage, but I prewash anyway to make sure the PUL doesn't do anything crazy like delaminate when washed. I've heard tales of purchasing PUL, spending forever making a diaper, and then having it delaminate in the first wash. It's rare, but it has happened. And while you might be able to return the fabric, you'll never be able to get your time back.

What this all boils down to is that hot cycles will typically be fine for washing cloth products. Just keep an eye on the wash instructions for your particular diapers, or if you're sewing, check the instructions on your fabrics.

For detergent, you must use cloth-diaper-friendly detergent, but this does not mean you need to buy specialty detergent. There are plenty of detergents available at the grocery store that you can use. The Diaper Jungle offers a chart to help you find safe detergents.

Some detergents include fabric softener, which can make water repel off the diapers. This can be disastrous and will require you to strip your diapers to make them usable again (more on stripping in a bit). For example, fabric softener can make your inserts stop absorbing liquid waste—it will just dribble out of the diaper. If your diapers are leaking, this could be the issue. Similarly, using too much detergent can cause the same problem. You should use the required amount only, and you must make sure your detergent is rinsed out well.

High-efficiency (HE) machines and non-HE machines do wash differently, but I have an HE machine and have found I'm able to successfully wash my cloth diapers in it. Your water type can also affect your wash routine.

Here's my routine:
1. Quick wash on cold: This rinses out all the solid and liquid waste. I do **not** add detergent to this portion of the cycle. I've heard using a hot or warm rinse could "set" the stains in the diaper, so I avoid that,

plus using cold for this rinse saves on electricity.
2. Wash with laundry detergent: I add detergent to my machine and wash on hot, heavy soiled, and high-speed spin.
3. Dry: Line drying is awesome and possibly better for your diapers, but I typically use my dryer. I put the diapers on medium heat for about 60 minutes. If my diapers are still wet, I will throw them in for 20 more minutes on high heat. If you have any stains, sunlight is the key to getting them out. Put the diapers out in the sun to dry, and the stains will magically disappear.

I've found inserts don't always dry on medium heat; if needed, I pull out the diaper shells and leave the inserts in the dryer on high for a bit longer.

Make sure to use HE detergent in an HE machine. If you have a front-loading machine, you should leave the door open after every use to air the interior out, but this isn't due to the diapers; front-loading machines get a bit musty smelling if you close the door between uses.

Clean washer following a cloth product wash cycle.

For more information on washing cloth diapers, I recommend checking out FluffLove University's How to Wash Cloth Diapers. They get into a lot of detail about detergent, water, and machine types so you can figure out the exact routine that's best for your family.

Here is a photo of my washing machine's interior immediately after a load of diapers was transferred into the dryer. As you can see, the machine is clean. If you properly rinse your diapers, you should have no issues with your machine getting dirty.

Stripping

Stripping is something that you can do to increase the absorbency of some portions of your diapers. Pocket shells and covers generally don't need to be stripped, but there are circumstances in which inserts may start repelling water and need to be stripped. I've only stripped my diapers once or twice in my whole cloth diapering experience. If you get the right routine and the right detergent, you likely won't need to strip your diapers. If you do need to, check out FluffLove University's article on [How to Strip Your Cloth Diapers](#).

Getting Rid of Stains

Stains aren't a big deal and are more of a vanity issue than anything else. If you're trying to resell items, particularly cloth diapers, you need to get rid of stains in order to increase resale value.

First, STEP AWAY FROM THE BLEACH!

Yes, bleach is great for getting rid of stains, and it's great for sanitizing your diapers if you bought them used. But I want to give you a better option that uses no chemicals and will cost you absolutely nothing.

After washing your diapers, set up a clothesline in your backyard and hang them up to dry in the bright sun. The limitation of this is that you need a nice sunny day, but nothing has ever bleached my diapers as well as the sun does. I love how easy it is, too—no scrubbing, no extra work. I just wash my diapers as normal, then lay them out in the sun to dry.

If you live in a community that forbids line drying clothing, check with your local laws to see if you have a "right to dry." For example, Maryland has a right to dry law, which means that you can't be forbidden from using a line to dry your clothing. We lived in a condo for a while that forbid the use of lines, and I eventually discovered that they couldn't legally do that. Line drying clothing or cloth diapers is much more environmentally friendly than using a dryer, so it's nice to see laws protecting that right.

Washing Reusable Products Without Electricity

I haven't had many opportunities to experiment with washing cloth products without electricity, but we once had a power outage for a few days, and I found that it is possible to wash by hand. I will briefly address this, but there are probably better people to ask than me if you plan to live off the grid!

We rinsed all of our diapers in the toilet (we are on city water so we still had the ability to flush) and flushed the solid waste. I can't attest to how you'd want to take care of this if you are homesteading and don't have plumbing, or if you are on well water. After rinsing, I put them in a bathtub full of water to soak. After soaking, I emptied the water and refilled the tub with soap and water. I scrubbed the diapers clean, rinsed with clean water, then hung them out to dry. I cleaned my tub after as well. I really wish I'd had a washing board during this process—it would have sped things up considerably.

If you plan to live off the grid, you can always purchase a small washing machine that doesn't require electricity.

Special Warnings

There are many things that can affect the absorbency of your cloth, and you need to be cautious not to use them.

Here are some things to beware of:

1. Diaper rash cream: Many common types of diaper rash cream can cause fabric to repel liquids. Make sure you use a cloth-diaper-friendly cream or spray, and if you need something more intense, you can use a liner or disposables for a few days until the rash clears up.
2. Too much detergent: Less is more. Adding extra detergent won't make your diapers cleaner. Use the required amount for your washing machine.
3. Fabric softener causes fabric to lose its absorbency. Make sure you aren't using dryer sheets or a detergent with fabric softener in it. Wool dryer balls are an ecofriendly alternative to fabric softener, and they'll also save you money if you stop buying dryer sheets.
4. Some fabrics will take a few washes before they gain full absorbency. For example, I made flannel wipes and unpaper towels recently, and they didn't initially absorb as well as my older ones. Some people like to run them through the wash until they have increased absorbency, but I usually just deal with it and only wash them after they have been used.

3 Types of Reusable Cloth Products

Cloth Diapers

Cloth diapers are an excellent alternative to disposable diapers. They're less likely to have issues with diaper explosions due to the elastic along the back of the diaper, and they come in many different fabrics. They tend to make your child's butt bigger as they're thicker than a disposable diaper, so you may need to size up on pants, but cloth diapers make an excellent cushion for when your baby falls!

I explain a little more about the different types of cloth diapers available in my video All About Cloth Diapering.

For a quick rundown, here are some different types of cloth diaper styles:

AIO or All-in-One

AIO diapers are similar to pocket diapers because they have a waterproof PUL exterior; however, unlike pocket diapers, the absorbency is not inserted into a pocket. Instead, inserts are sewn into the "wet zone" of the diaper. They have to be washed after one use.

AI2 or All-in-Two

This diaper is similar to an AIO, but the insert lays on top or is snapped into the diaper. Since only the insert is impacted, you remove the insert to launder and replace it with a new insert. You can reuse the shell of the diaper until it gets wet or dirty. AI2 diapers are appealing because you don't have to do as much laundry, but you will frequently find that it's a rare occasion that the shell doesn't also get soiled once your child is on the go.

Pocket Diapers

Pocket diapers don't need a cover or a prefold. They are a complete diaper and are very similar to a disposable diaper. Some are made with hook and loop, while others are made with snaps. They have a pocket in the back of the diaper where you put an insert for absorbency. Most pocket diapers are sold with the insert, but you can also buy them separately. You stuff your insert into the pocket; if your baby is a heavy wetter, you can add extra inserts for more absorbency. Many pocket diapers retail with a microfiber insert, but microfiber cannot touch your baby's skin because it can cause a rash. The pocket diaper leaves a layer of fabric between your baby and the insert to prevent this issue. The microfiber inserts aren't too bulky and have good absorbency. The drawback to this diaper type is that you have to stuff the inserts back in after you wash and dry them. This type of diaper needs to be washed after every use.

Prefolds

This is the kind of diaper that your grandparents secured with pins. It's flat and has a ton of absorbency. The prefold itself holds in the pee and the poop, and a cover or pants keeps the wet fabric away from baby's clothes—and contains anything that escapes from the prefold. Owning a lot of prefolds and a few covers is the cheapest option for cloth diapering. I have seen good-quality prefolds for $1–2 each. However, you need to fold them to put them on your child, so I struggled to use them once my kids were old enough to make diaper changes difficult. Also, you need prefolds in the right size for your child.

You can use a Snappi to secure the prefold on the baby with an attractive cover over it. Prefolds are easy to upcycle for other uses because of how absorbent and easy to clean they are.

Fitted Diapers

Fitted diapers need a cover over them if you want them to be leak resistant. They have elastic on the legs and back, and some people put snaps or a hook and loop on to hold them together. For fitted diapers without a closure built in, you can use a Snappi. I have made fitted diapers out of old t shirts, and some people make them out of prefolds. They're slightly easier to use than the prefold because they don't require special folding. Fitted diapers need to be washed after every use.

Covers

Back in the day, parents used rubber pants as covers for prefolds. Now you can use cute diaper covers that are made with PUL, wool, or other liquid-resistant fabrics. You must purchase a separate item to go inside the covers for absorbency (a fitted diaper or a prefold). Covers don't need to be washed unless pee or poop gets on the cover. You can often just take a wet cloth to wipe down the inside of the cover so you can reuse it immediately. This results in less washing, as well as less wear and tear on the diapers covers.

Wool Covers

Some people knit, crochet, or sew wool sweaters to make a cover. These covers are usually called "longies" or "shorties" depending on if they're worn as pants or shorts. Like PUL covers, they are only washed if they get dirty, and they are used over an absorbent diaper.

Training Underwear

Training underwear is similar to a pull up. Training underwear will have slightly less absorbency than a cloth diaper and will be easy for your child to get on and off. It has an interior liner that is next to your child's skin and should not wick liquid waste into the liner—you want your child to feel the wetness.

Diapers for Pets and Adults

Just to touch on this briefly, you can also make or buy cloth diapers for pets or adults. People make them for dogs, goats, chickens, and other animals. They are also useful for adults or older children who have disabilities or medical problems. With babies and toddlers, there's usually an end in sight for your diapering experience, but for animals or people who need to use diapers long term, you can save a lot of money by using cloth and save the environment while helping to make someone (or yourself) more comfortable!

Cloth Wipes and Family Cloth

Cloth wipes are an alternative to disposable wipes, and many people prefer them because they are chemical-free. You can just wet them with water to wipe your child, or can make your own wipe solution. I prefer using plain water.

I've tried a couple of options for designing my cloth wipes; two-ply flannel (two layers of flannel sewn together) is my favorite because it absorbs water quickly and easily, the fabric is affordable and cute, and the wipes are easy to use.

Completed nursing pads

You can use a cloth wipe as a wash cloth, burp cloth, napkin, handkerchief, and more. I often give them as baby shower gifts because they've gotten rave reviews, even from non-cloth-diapering friends.

Nursing Pads

Completed cloth wipes

Nursing pads are used for the early stages of breastfeeding (or the entire time you breastfeed, depending on your body) to prevent milk from leaking through your bra onto your shirt. Super glamorous stuff, motherhood. I have used both disposable and reusable nursing pads. I find that the disposable nursing pads irritate my skin, similar to disposable menstrual pads, but they aren't quite so obvious under my shirt. Reusable nursing pads tend to be a bit more obvious, but I've found them to be more comfortable, and I figure that nobody should be looking that hard at my breasts. My face is up here, people!

You can buy or make flat or contoured nursing pads, but I prefer flat. Some people find that they are able to hide the contoured ones better under their shirts, but I've got a relatively flat chest, and the contoured pads make me look like a robot from a crazy science fiction movie.

Unpaper Towels

I feel silly even mentioning unpaper towels because they're really what our parents and grandparents just called "kitchen towels." They're not exactly a new thing. I have plenty of kitchen towels, but I make unpaper towels with two layers of flannel, sizing them to be about the same size as a paper towel. I'm more likely to grab the unpaper towels for cleaning up messes and use my kitchen towels for drying dishes.

Completed unpaper towels.

There are a lot of benefits to using these instead of paper towels or a sponge. I like doing clean up with them because they go immediately into the wash after use and don't grow bacteria like a sponge will. They also have a longer lifespan than a sponge.

I really appreciate these when my sons like to help clean up—they'll grab a hand full of towels to do a small job. This would be an expensive habit if they were using paper towels. With unpaper towels, there's no expense, and they learn to help. I frequently give them a squirt bottle full of water (labeled with their name on it) and an unpaper towel to wash our sliding glass door or windows.

Some people like to add snaps to their unpaper towels and then snap them together in a roll, similar to paper towels. I tried this for my first set and it seemed like a huge waste of time. Now I just lay them on top of one another and store them in a drawer. This way, it's much less time consuming to put them away once they're dry.

Handkerchiefs

Handkerchiefs are a relatively new item that I've been exploring since my husband requested that I make them. Remembering to use them instead of tissues has been a weird adjustment for me, but they are a lot more comfortable. As a bonus, if I'm sick and my nose is really red, I can wet the handkerchiefs before using them.

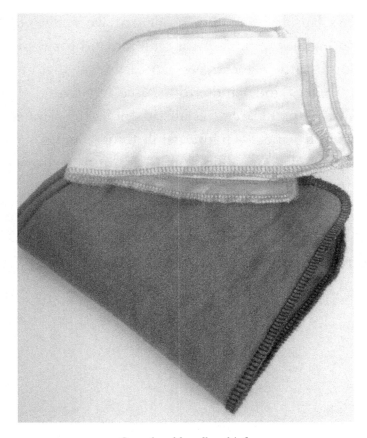

Completed handkerchiefs.

I need to make a lot more if we ever plan to use these in place of tissues, but I'm still exploring my various options for fabrics to use to make them, as well as the size I prefer.

Napkins

Fabric napkins are nothing new, but I make them in small squares instead of the size of the bigger cloth napkins that you would typically use on your lap. The smaller squares mean less laundry, and they're all that we really need for regular use. They're perfect for children and for wiping our own mouths after we eat. We can easily wet them to wipe our boys' faces and hands, too. Also, I've found that the large fabric napkins aren't as absorbent as the flannel I use for our cloth wipes—children spill things, and it's nice to have a quick cleanup option (although unpaper towels can do the trick, too).

We save the large fabric napkins for more formal dinners.

Menstrual Pads (Mama Cloth)

Completed reusable menstrual pad.

Fabric menstrual pads are *definitely* the item that I said I would never use because it was "gross." A few years later, I'm a complete convert—foot in mouth. I love my reusable menstrual pads. They save a lot of money and don't irritate me like disposables do. They're also not much extra to wash because they are such a small item. I throw them in with the cloth diapers.

My favorite part is that they are soft, so they're super comfortable to wear. They also stay on better due to the snap I use to hold them on. I've been amazed at how much money I have saved using them. I think my husband doesn't truly appreciate how much money I save using fabric products because he's never had to buy feminine products or excessive amounts of toilet paper until he married me.

For tampon users, you can go green and save money by using the Diva Cup or a similar product. I'm not a fan of tampons, so I haven't tried an alternative yet. My friend loves her Diva Cup, though, and we have discussed ways to use them if you'll be out for a long time and need to empty it. My suggestion was this: buy two Diva Cups and keep a clean one inside a clean and zippered wet bag in your purse. When you need to empty the one you're currently using, remove it and empty it into the toilet. Take the clean one from your purse to use and place the used one into the now empty wet bag, zipper, and keep it until later so you can wash it at home. I have heard the Diva Cup works for up to 10 hours, but I'm guessing this might be useful for people who have long shifts at work or very heavy cycles.

Cloth Swim Diapers

Cloth swim diapers, like disposable swim diapers or regular cloth diapers, have elastic that is tight around the legs and back, so you don't have to deal with any escaping waste into the pool. None of these will prevent true diarrhea from escaping though, so make sure to avoid pools when your child is sick.

Regular cloth diaper shells that fit well on your child will work just fine for the pool; we just remove the inserts and use the pocket shell. You should not use your inserts in the pool, so AIO diapers are not a good option.

The one problem with using your normal cloth diapers in the pool is that the chlorine may damage them. As a result, many people opt to purchase a dedicated cloth swim diaper or just make sure not to use a favorite cloth diaper.

Someone is going to jump in here and say it's gross that kids are peeing in the pool if you don't use absorbency. That was my initial thought, too, until someone pointed out that any absorbency is going to absorb the pool water *way* before it absorbs urine. Also, too much absorbency could be a drowning risk as it would weigh a child down in the water. Yikes! So keep in mind that your disposable swim diapers aren't doing anything more or less than a cloth swim diaper would, although some disposable or cloth swim diapers offer a small amount of absorbency that may allow you to put one on before you drive to the pool so that if they pee, it won't flood the car seat. I would not trust one, however, to protect my car seat and think it's a good idea to wait until you get to the pool to change into a swim diaper.

Wet Bags

I think everyone should own a wet bag. They are so useful, particularly if you are going to the gym or pool. They're a great way to contain sweaty gym clothes until you get home. They can contain dirty cloth diapers, wet swimsuits, dirty unpaper towels, and dirty handkerchiefs.

A wet bag made of one layer of PUL and a matching snack bag.

Wet bags can be made or bought in different sizes, depending on your needs. Most have a zipper that allows them to contain smells, and they are made with water-resistant PUL, which keeps wetness from leaking through the bag.

Because they're made with PUL, they can be put through the wash when you get home. You need to open the zipper so both the inside of the bag and the clothes inside will get clean. Removing the clothing and flipping the bag inside out works best.

Wet bags are water resistant, which is slightly different than waterproof. You can't put a soaking wet diaper or swimsuit inside the wet bag and expect it to hold the water, but if you wring out the diaper or swimsuit before placing it in the bag, the wetness will not leak through. Normally diapers are fine in a wet bag without being wrung out unless they are soaked with water.

A small wet bag will work for one or two diapers on the go, or a couple swimsuits. You'll want a medium-sized bag if you're putting a lot of gym clothes into one. Large and extra-large wet bags are great for storing cloth diapers until you're ready to wash them.

We always take two or three small or medium wet bags when we go on vacation so we can store any bad messes in a zippered bag until we get home. Recently we went on vacation and one of our children had an accident. I quickly rinsed the pair of jeans, let them dry, and then zipped them up in the bag until we got home so I could wash them. It worked well even though we were gone for an entire week.

Having a wet bag also allows us to swim on last day of vacation. We just wring out the wet swimsuits and place them in the wet bag until we get home.

Refrigerator Liners

My refrigerator liner in action.

In the past, I've lined my refrigerator shelves with plastic wrap to help make cleaning up easier. You remove the plastic wrap when you need to clean up and then throw it away. I wasn't happy with it because it wasn't ecofriendly. Instead, I made some easy reusable liners for my refrigerator, and I love them! The liners are thick enough to offer great coverage, they're easy to make, and they store well. The PUL can also be washed on a hot cycle to kill bacteria.

I have two sets. They're easier and faster to apply than plastic wrap. Since they're made from PUL only, they don't absorb liquids, but the texture prevents small amounts of liquid from running off the shelf onto other levels of the refrigerator. To apply my liners, I wipe down a shelf with a wet sponge so it's slightly wet. Then I stick a liner, shiny side of the PUL down, onto the shelf. It sticks pretty well.

Reusable Snack Bags

Completed reusable snack bag.

Reusable snack bags are a relatively new item I've started making. I use food-safe PUL for mine, and I like how easily they fold up when you're done with them. They're easier to store than a reusable plastic or glass storage container, and I was very excited to find another use for my beautiful PUL fabric.

Fabric Gift Bags

Cloth gift bags will probably be your favorite cloth item because they're never gross and don't need washed. They also make wrapping presents easy. If you want to refresh them, you can wash or iron them. I usually run ours through the dryer with a wet washcloth to refresh them and remove wrinkles.

They are also really convenient. During Christmas this year, I was excited to have so many because it took us a quarter of the time to put all the gifts under the tree. You simply find the right size bag, place your gift inside, and pull the drawstring closed. You can attach a tag with ribbon. I was also pleased to see that Amazon was wrapping their gifts in fabric bags this year—they looked really nice and were worth the money.

Our Christmas tree this year. We still wrapped a few items.

4 Storage Solutions for Reusable Cloth

Cloth Diapers

Storing cloth diapers is always a fun challenge, and people approach it in many different ways. I like to store my cloth diapers with the inserts in them already. I use baskets mounted to the wall so the diapers are easily accessible. Some people put them in drawers. Others use large shoe organizers that hang over the back of a door.

Baskets that we mounted to the wall for our cloth diaper storage.

Cloth Wipes, Cloth Napkins, and Handkerchiefs

These are all the same approximate size, so you can store them in the same way. I usually store my cloth wipes stacked on top of each other in a little basket, but I've folded them in half to stack on a shelf as well. I've found they also fit well in a magazine holder that attaches to the side of the toilet. Cloth napkins can go inside a napkin holder.

Unpaper Towels

I stack my unpaper towels inside a drawer in my kitchen, but other people use snaps or hook and loop to connect them. If you do that, you can wind them around a paper towel holder and structure them more like disposable paper towels. I, however, find this approach time consuming, so it's not my cup of tea. You can also use a nice basket on the counter to hold them.

Cloth napkins in a napkin holder.

Cloth napkins stored in baskets.

Unpaper towels stored in a basket.

Wet Bags

I store my wet bags folded in a drawer or under the bathroom sink until I need them, but this is how I hang them in my sons' bathroom when they're in use. I love this option because we use the other hooks for towels.

The handle on the wet bag can also fit over a door knob if it's made big enough.

Wet bag hanging in our bathroom.

Mama Cloth or Cloth Menstrual Pads

You can keep a small bag in the bathroom next to a wet bag to store clean mama cloth in. I bought some fabric bins for the shelves above our toilet, and I store my mama cloth in the lowest bin so it's easy to reach.

Storage solutions in our bathroom.

5 Preparing to Sew Cloth Diapers

Choosing a Pattern

The first step is to decide on a pattern. I use a one-size pocket pattern for the bulk of my cloth diaper stash.

I usually sew a few newborn covers and buy newborn-size prefolds with Snappis to get through the initial month (remember, prefold-style diapers require a cover). My babies have all been big, so they've transitioned to one-size diapers fairly fast. It's not worth it to me to purchase or sew a lot of newborn diapers. Also, I find that prefolds with covers are more difficult to put on a wiggly toddler, but they're easy (once you understand how) to put on a newborn. Using prefolds early on also helps to save some money since prefolds are cheap and you only need a few covers. Due to the smaller size of the newborn covers, I can also make them out of scrap fabric that is left over from making the one-size stash.

Purchasing a great diaper pattern is a worthwhile investment, but I use the free patterns from Simple Diaper Sewing Tutorials frequently. I liked how the XL pattern fit my older sons, and I'm hoping the one-size and newborn-cover patterns fit just as well.

That said, you may want to try several different patterns. Some diaper patterns fit certain children better than others.

Your baby's leg size and gender are just two factors that can influence the overall fit of a cloth diaper. That's not to say you're going to be absolutely screwed if you sew diapers from a pattern that doesn't fit your baby perfectly—most one-size patterns will do the trick, and you can also adjust the leg elastics to make a diaper fit better. But I've noticed many cloth diaper users have a particular diaper fit they love best, so if you feel like experimenting, get a few different patterns and make some of each. This does, however, require more math when you calculate your supplies.

Choosing Your Supplies

Buying supplies to sew an entire cloth diaper stash can be intimidating, but it can also be fun.

It can be intimidating because you must figure out the math ahead of time to ensure you get enough supplies. But choosing fabric is fun—I recommend waiting until you know the baby's gender because you may want to choose your fabrics based on that. If you want to get a head start, however, you can make absorbency layers early in pregnancy, or you can stick with a gender-neutral diaper stash.

I'm going to try to break this down to make it easier to understand. I have sewn three full diaper stashes: two sets of one-size diapers and one set of XL diapers when my sons outgrew the one-size pattern. Keep in mind that most one-size diaper patterns seem to run through 30 lbs, and you may or may not have a potty trained child by then depending on your child's age, potty training, and growth rate. My sons both potty trained on the later side and grew quickly.

The first step is to decide how many diapers you want to make. Newborns go through diapers much faster than do older babies. How many diapers you want also depends on how frequently you want to wash and what type of diaper you choose. Covers can be reused if you just change out the prefold or fitted diaper underneath, unless they get poop on them. Pocket and AIO diapers need to be washed after every change. And AI2 diapers are similar to covers with prefolds because you can swap out the absorbency and reuse the cover for pee changes.

I'm going to focus on pocket diapers as they seem to be the popular and easy choice for cloth diapering newbies. It's also what I'll be sewing.

A young baby will go through 10–15 diapers a day, depending on how diligent you are about changing. I've heard some new moms say they're changing their babies more than that, likely because we tend to worry more as new parents.

I don't think it's great to go more than two or three days between washing cloth diapers. So I would plan on sewing at least 24 one-size diapers. You can certainly sew more if you want, but don't let dirty diapers sit in a wet bag for two weeks just because you have 80 diapers.

I'll sew five newborn covers and buy 24 newborn prefolds. While I could sew my own prefolds, they're reasonably priced, and I like to use my time wisely. (If you're on a tight budget, there are also some more economical ways to sew diapers. I'll talk more about that later.)

Supply List:

- PUL for the exterior
- An interior stay-dry fabric that wicks away moisture: minky, suedecloth, microfleece, or athletic wicking jersey, for example
- Absorbency fabric for the inserts: bamboo, cotton, hemp, or microfiber, for example
- Snaps for adjusting the rise of the diapers
- Snap pliers
- Snaps or hook-and-loop closure for adjusting the waist of the diaper (the "tabs" and the strip across the front of the diaper)
- Elastic for the leg holes and back of the diaper

Exterior Fabrics

PUL fabric is the most commonly used exterior fabric because it can be washed in hot water. If you want to save money, buy solid-color PUL; patterned PUL is more expensive. (Some people use wool as an exterior fabric, but that's more relevant for covers.)

Stay-Dry Fabric

Consider using a couple different types of stay-dry fabric for your diapers. I mention this because this is the part of the diaper that touches your baby's skin. Some babies get rashes from contact with certain fabrics; it's not common, but it's possible. Having multiple types of fabric for the interiors of your diapers will help you troubleshoot whether any issues are related to fabric choice.

Absorbency Fabric

You can mix and match fabrics for the inserts. Each type of absorbency fabric is a little different. Depending on the type of fabric, you'll need to use more or fewer layers.

A lot of the early pocket diapers came with microfiber inserts, but many manufacturers are using other fabrics now. I like natural fibers because microfiber can cause rashes in some babies if it comes into contact with their skin. The ability to use my inserts in an AI2 diaper if desired also gives me more flexibility, and I just don't like the feel of microfiber.

Snaps and Snap Pliers or Press

KamSnaps is one of the bigger suppliers for snaps and snap pliers; you can buy their items in a variety of online stores. I find their pliers work well and last.

Many people opt for a snap press rather than snap pliers. I have never used a snap press, so I can't attest to the convenience of one versus the other, but I like the size and portability of the pliers. For the purpose of making a stash for yourself, pliers will do the trick.

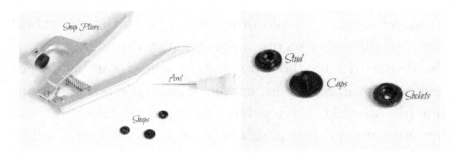

Left, tools for installing snaps; the snap pliers close the snaps and the awl is for creating a hole in your fabric to poke the snap through. Right, a cap is required for each stud or socket.

Snaps vs. Hook and Loop

Cloth diapers use two types of closures: snaps and hook and loop. When you're looking into making the diapers, you want to consider which type of closure you'll want. There are benefits to both. If you opt for hook and loop, you'll still need some snaps and snap pliers to put the rise adjustments on one-size diapers.

Hook and loop is easy to use, and it makes your pocket diaper similar to a disposable, making it easier for family and daycare providers to use them.

Left, tools for installing snaps; the snap pliers close the snaps and the awl is for creating a hole in your fabric to poke the snap through. Right, a cap is required for each stud or socket.

Hook refers to the scratchy portion and loop refers to the soft portion. When you're sewing it on, the hook portion needs to be on the tabs. The loop is sewn across the front of the diaper. You do not want to put hook along the front because hook has a special way of attracting fuzz and other stuff like waste…and it's not pretty. Due to this issue, hook-and-loop diapers should have a laundry tab. Closing the hook tab on a laundry tab will help prevent fuzz from building up in the hook, and it keeps the hook from grabbing on your PUL or liner, which can damage the fabric. Some wear and tear to hook and loop is normal over time, though, regardless of how well you care for it.

Snaps are the best option for the longevity of a diaper because they don't generally need to be replaced. The other benefit to snaps is that they make the diaper more difficult for a child to pull off. Hook and loop is easier to figure out, so if you have a child who likes to rip their diaper off to play naked in their poop, you may want to opt for snaps. My sons did not ever try to pull off their diapers, however, and I thought the high-quality hook and loop that I used was difficult to remove.

Hook and loop is easier and faster to sew on, in my opinion. Snaps require you to add additional PUL squares or strips to help support the snaps and prevent them from pulling through the diaper. I know this probably doesn't sell you on snaps. I started with an entire one-size stash of snap diapers, and the snaps added a lot of time to the diaper-making process. I also tend to have issues with wrist pain, so applying all of the snaps was brutal. As such, my personal preference is hook and loop.

In terms of being more ecofriendly, I'd lean more toward snaps because the diaper will last longer without needing the hook and loop replaced. Also, snaps can be easy to apply while watching your favorite TV show or movie. You need to be at a sewing machine to apply hook and loop.

Calculating Your Supplies

To calculate your supplies, you'll need to have your pattern printed out and put together. You'll want to measure the length of the diaper and the width at the widest part (this should be the back of the diaper). This will tell you the size cut of fabric you'll need for one diaper. You'll need this size cut in both the PUL exterior and the stay-dry interior.

Keep in mind that your fabric needs to be cut so its stretch goes across the width of the diaper, not the length. If your fabric pattern is plain or multidirectional, you can flip the diaper pattern from top to bottom to squeeze more cuts out of each yard of fabric.

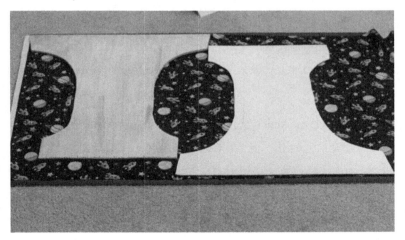

You can squeeze more diaper cuts across the width of fabric if you can flip the pattern upside down, but this is dependent on the fabric being bidirectional.

I order a lot of my diaper fabric and supplies from Diaper Sewing Supplies. I'm sure there are other good options and stores, but I like the patterns and cut sizes they offer. Their online store currently allows you to buy PUL in the following sizes: by the yard, as a diaper cut (20 in by 20 in), 20 in by the full width of the fabric, or 22 in by the full width of the fabric. My pattern requires me to buy the 22 in cut or to purchase by the yard.

Example Measurements

Let's calculate measurements using the long wing, one-size square tab pattern from Simple Diaper Sewing Tutorials as an example. When I put my pattern together, I measured the length and width as 20.5 in by 18.5 in. This means that I cannot use the 20 in options from Diaper Sewing Supplies. I like to purchase the 22 in option because it's cheaper than a full yard, and I don't want a lot of diapers with the same pattern. The width of this fabric is 55–56 in, so I can get up to three diaper cuts from this strip if I'm careful.

Stay-dry fabric is sold by the yard. You can calculate how many cuts you'll get by looking at your fabric's measurements. I really like the feel of microfleece, a yard of which is 36 in long and 60–62 in wide. For a 20.5 in diaper, I can only fit one cut on a yard from top to bottom, then several diapers across. The best way to get the most for your money is to purchase two yards (uncut), which gives you 72 in of height. I can fit three heights worth of cuts onto two yards of fabric and then three across. This means I can make nine cloth diapers from two yards of the microfleece with a minimal amount of microfleece waste.

Your pattern should also include the number of snaps you'll need and show the elastic casing area. For the long-wing, one-size square tab pattern, I would need 32 snaps for each snaps-only diaper (not adding the snap for the insert or umbilical snap down as I do not use those).

Snaps come in studs (male), sockets (female), and caps; I usually use sockets across the front and studs for the tabs. The top snaps for the rise are studs, and the bottom ones are sockets. In this case, you'll want eight studs and 24 sockets per diaper. Note that each stud and socket requires a cap, so you need 32 caps.

If you opt for hook and loop, you'll still need two studs, four sockets, and six caps per diaper. You'll want 9.75 in width of loop for the front, a total of 4 in (2 in each) of loop for the laundry tabs, and 4 in (2 in each) of hook for the tabs. If you want overlapping tabs, you'll need an additional 2–4 in of loop. For the purpose of these calculations, I only used 2 in of loop for overlapping.

For the leg elastic, you can measure the width of the casings that are shown on your pattern. In this example, the casing is approximately 9 in for the back and 11.5 in per side, which means I will need 32 in of leg elastic per diaper.

For this example, I'm not going to calculate anything for inserts. We'll talk more about inserts when I get to the section about sewing inserts.

My Supplies

I decided to make 24 one-size cloth diapers with hook and loop, one overlapping tab with loop, and a snap-down rise. I did my calculations accordingly.

Here's the list for what I need. If you decide to use my numbers, please carefully check the math, your pattern, and your fabric dimensions because all of those things can change the calculated numbers.

- PUL 22-in cuts: I need 8 (no extra fabric remaining); I ordered 12 because you have to cut very carefully to be sure to get 3 per cut and I needed to make other items as well
- Microfleece: 6 yards
- Snaps: 48 male snaps, 96 female snaps, 144 caps
- Elastic: 768 in or 22 yards; I recommend adding a few yards to your order in case you mess up—I ordered 30 yards
- Hook: 96 in
- Loop: 378 in

It's never a bad thing to order a bit too much elastic or hook and loop to account for mistakes. As stated above, I did order more PUL than I needed.

The hard part is calculating how much you'll need of each color for hook, loop, stay-dry fabric, and snaps, considering you'll likely want to mix and match with your PUL selections. But this gives you a general idea of the amounts you'll need.

To give you an idea of the cost of this project, it cost me roughly $9/diaper for my supplies, although I did not cut costs at all when it came to ordering, and I will have extra of some stuff, such as the PUL.

How to Make a Wood Pattern Form

When I first started making cloth diapers, my brother made me a wood pattern form that made cutting out my fabric quicker. To make the pattern form, you'll need your pattern, some thin wood (thin plywood or balsa would work) or hardboard, and a jigsaw. You'll also need safety gear.

Lay the wood down and trace the paper pattern on to the wood. Be careful not to let the paper pattern shift.

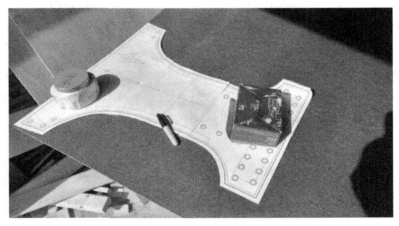

Making a wood pattern form.

Once you've traced the paper pattern, use your jig saw to cut it out. Make sure to use safety equipment and clamp your board in place so it won't shift. Please take the time to review the safety and use guidelines for your jigsaw.

Jigsaw about to cut out the wood pattern form.

Once you've cut the patterns out, you can sand down any rough edges to keep them from catching on fabric. Make sure to lay your paper pattern back over the wood form to ensure you cut the pattern correctly. I cut one from thin plywood and another from hardboard. You can opt to use a drill to create the holes for marking your snap placement, but I use my paper pattern for transferring those markings.

HOW TO SEW, USE, AND CLEAN CLOTH DIAPERS

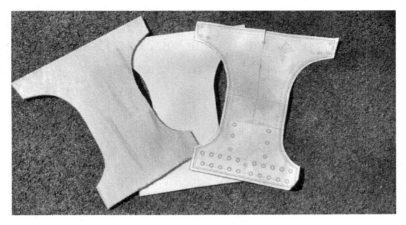

Completed pattern forms.

Sewing an Entire Stash Fast

When you're sewing a diaper here and there, you don't worry too much about speed. Most people, however, are attempting to sew an entire stash of cloth diapers when they get started.

First, I recommend making one or two first to make sure you understand the process. You don't want to mess up 24 diapers all at once.

Once you've gotten the basic idea down, you can set up an assembly line. You want to complete one task at a time for all of the diapers you're making. This is mind numbing, but it saves quite a bit of time because you're not scrambling for supplies for each step each time you make a diaper. You can cut all of your interior and exterior fabrics at once, then move on to adding your snaps or hook and loop. This also allows you to keep your machine settings the same as you sew (e.g., I zig-zag my hook and loop on).

I'll get into more specific details on the process in the next chapter, but first I will outline an example assembly line method you may want to use for different styles of diapers: hook-and-loop one-size diapers; snap-closure one-size diapers; and sized diapers.

Hook-and-Loop One-Size Diapers

Step 1: Wash all fabric before beginning.

Step 2: Cut interior and exterior fabric for the diapers. Make sure the fabric's stretch is across the waistline.

Step 3: Sew the loop on to the front of the PUL diaper cut.

Step 4: Add the snap-down rise. Make sure to reinforce the snaps with an additional piece of fabric (on the wrong side of the PUL).

Step 5: Make the pocket on the interior fabric cuts.

Step 6: Pin and sew the interior and exterior fabric cuts, right sides together.

Step 7: Turn and top stitch.

Step 8: Mark all of your casing locations using a temporary fabric marker or chalk.

Step 9: Sew the casings.

Step 10: Add the elastic.

Step 11: Sew the hook tabs and loop laundry tabs on to the diaper.

Snap-Closure One-Size Diapers

It's the same process as the hook-and-loop one-size diapers, except step 3 is to place all of the snaps, and step 11 is to add male snaps as a closure for the diapers.

My suggestion for snapping diapers is to further break down the assembly line and glue on some backing in the snap area to reinforce where the snaps will go. Then mark all of the spots for snaps; you can poke the holes through with your awl, then add snaps. It's pretty time consuming, but the more you break it down, the faster it will go.

Sized Diapers

Sized diapers are very similar, except you skip the snap-down rise.

Time Commitment for Sewing Diapers Assembly-Line Style

Snap One-Size Diapers With Welt Pocket

These were the numbers I came up with when sewing my all-snap one-size diapers a few years ago. I did include a welt pocket, which is a slightly slower process than how I do pockets now. (A welt pocket is a pocket that is set in to a diaper or piece of clothing. Compare this to its counterpart, the patch pocket, which is sewn on to clothing.) Keep in mind that I was newer to sewing, so that could have contributed some to my speed.

- Cut PUL for the exterior fabric: 3 min per diaper
- Cut fabric for welt pocket and interior fabric: 2.75 min per diaper
- Mark PUL for snap placement: 1.1 min per diaper
- Add snaps: 24.25 min per diaper
- Add welt pocket: 4.55 min per diaper
- Pin and sew right sides together, trim edges, flip right-side out: 8 min per diaper
- Top stitch: 3.5 min per diaper
- Mark and sew casings: 4 min per diaper
- Add elastic: 8–9 min per diaper
- Add last snaps: 4 min per diaper

Total time per diaper: 63 min

Hook-and-Loop Diapers Without the Welt Pocket

Because I needed to sew an entire new stash, I wanted to retry this experiment with the hook-and-loop method instead. I also skipped the welt pocket. Before you think that lazy is the right way to go, keep in mind that cloth diapers can last through several children, and they do have resale value. Each diaper may take time to make, but it can be worth the extra effort to make sure they come out right.

Personally, I'm happy with my non-welt pockets, but if you're really attached to welt pockets, then it's worth the extra time. After all, you'll see these diapers frequently over the next few years, so you want to love them. It's important to consider the payoff for time spent making the diapers, too, not to just rush through making them.

- Cut PUL: 1.34 min per diaper
- Cut interior fabric: 1.34 min per diaper
- Add hook and loop to front: 2.90 min per diaper
- Add snap rise: 6.13 min per diaper
- Cut and serge pocket: 1.26 min per diaper
- Pin and sew right sides together, flip right-side out: 6.6 min per diaper
- Top stitch: 4.83 min per diaper
- Mark and sew casings: 5 min per diaper
- Add elastic: 7.25 min per diaper
- Add hook closure and laundry tabs: 6 min per diaper

Total time per diaper: 42.65 min

6 How to Sew Cloth Diapers

How to Sew a Cloth Diaper With Pockets

Of all of the reusable fabric products, cloth diapers are the most complicated to sew. They were one of the first items I tried sewing when I got started, however, so it is possible to learn to sew them if you are an amateur seamstress. The key for sewing PUL is to use a walking foot on your sewing machine. You can sew diapers without one, but it's not as easy, so a walking foot is worth buying if you plan to make more than one or two diapers.

I'm going to go over how I make my pocket diapers. There are many options for how to make them, but I'm going to show you an extra-large size pocket diaper with hook-and-loop closures. I use casings for my elastic rather than sewing it down, and I sewed the hook-and-loop tabs partially off of the diaper. I also added laundry tabs to the diapers, and I have an easy cut for the pocket area. You can do all sorts of creative things with cloth diapers—embroider them, add ruffles, add a tail or other accessories, and more. You just need to work within the confines of your fabric choices.

My favorite website for diaper sewing tutorials and patterns is [Simple Diaper Sewing Tutorials](). The site offers many options for customizing cloth diapers so they work for you.

For this tutorial, I am using the [Pocket AIO Extra Large pattern]() from Simple Diaper Sewing Tutorials. I love this pattern for my sons; it fits them perfectly, and it's free. We started using these once my boys outgrew their one-size diapers. If you sew a one-size diaper, you will need to put additional snaps on for adjusting the front of the diaper. This part is called a snap-down rise.

Here's a photo of two diapers with the snap-down rise. The diaper on the right has the rise snapped down already. The open diaper on the left shows snaps across to adjust the waist, then the snap-down rise is below it. You can see one male snap and two female snaps under it. The male snaps can snap into the lowest female snaps for smaller babies, then you move up as the baby grows. Eventually you won't use the rise snaps at all once you reach the largest setting.

Diapers with a snap-down rise.

Tips on Needles and Thread

Use 100% polyester thread for sewing PUL. Also be aware that holes in PUL can cause leaks, so people who sew cloth diapers regularly are very careful about their needle selection. I've heard to use sizes 9 or 11 ballpoint or stretch needles, but it appears there is some disagreement on whether a ballpoint or a sharp needle is the better choice.

According to some, the sharper needles pierce the fabric better and the PUL heals better; these people prefer to use Microtex needles in size 10.

Personally, I use a universal needle because my machine loathes the ballpoint needles and skips stitches when I try to use one while sewing these diapers. I've seen people say they have no issues with using a universal needle, so I decided to go with it. The big thing to watch for is needle size—don't use bigger than a size 11 needle.

Step-by-Step Instructions

Step 1: Use a pattern to cut the exterior and interior fabric.

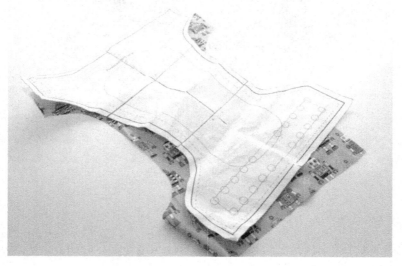

Cut fabric for a cloth diaper.

Comparison of Alova Suedecloth (green) vs. bubble minky interior fabric.

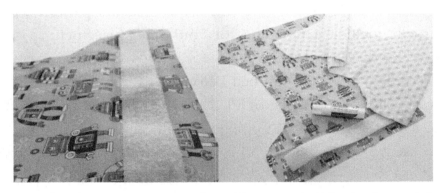

Left, using glue to hold the loop in place while you sew it. Right, the zig-zag stitch that I used for the loop on my diaper front.

Step 2: Use a glue stick to stick the loop on to the front of the diaper. This just helps hold it in place. Alternatively, you could pin it on. Sew the loop on to the front of the diaper with a zig-zag stitch and make sure it's secure.

Additional note for sewing one-size diapers: If you are sewing one-size diapers or a pattern that has rise snaps, you would add your snap down rise during this step.

When you add snaps, always reinforce them with an additional piece of fabric on the wrong sides of the fabric. This keeps the snaps from pulling through the PUL after the diapers have been used many times. I usually cut out squares of scrap PUL that are slightly larger than the snap cap and face the squares right sides together with the hole for the snap. The snap will go through both layers of PUL.

Using snaps instead of hook and loop: Some people use snaps instead of hook and loop for their cloth diapers. It's a matter of preference. If you use snaps, the pattern will usually include a template for your snap placement. You can mark where each snap goes, then add the snaps accordingly. As I mentioned before, always reinforce snaps with a little extra piece of PUL on the inside of the fabric to keep the snap from ripping through the fabric after a lot of use.

Step 3: Cut the pocket for the interior of the fabric. I used my rotary cutter to cut a strip along the top middle of the interior fabric. Then I turned the knife off on my serger and serged around the edges of the pocket area. I turned the edges under and sewed a straight stitch around it for a more finished look.

HOW TO SEW, USE, AND CLEAN CLOTH DIAPERS

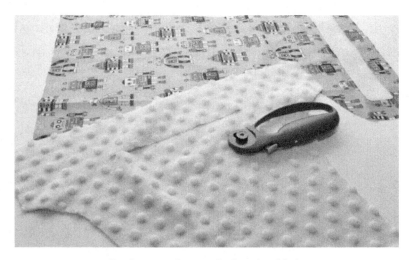

Cutting a pocket on the interior fabric.

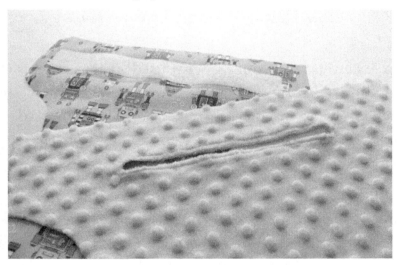

Finished edges of the pocket.

Step 4: Face the interior and exterior fabrics right sides together and pin or clip together. (Using clips helps prevent additional holes in the PUL.)

Interior and exterior fabric cut and pinned together.

Step 5: Sew around your diaper. I used a serger because it's faster and I like how it looks. But a straight stitch on a normal sewing machine is fine, too. Make sure to pay attention to the seam allowance for your pattern and leave the correct amount.

I find that sewing or serging with the PUL side up is easier than sewing with the stretchy interior fabric side up. If you sew with the interior side up, the fabric can stretch out a bit during the process and it looks bad. That said, the slippery side of PUL can be difficult to sew with a sewing machine; this is why a walking foot is a good investment. It will make the process a lot faster and easier. My serger foot has no problems with PUL, however.

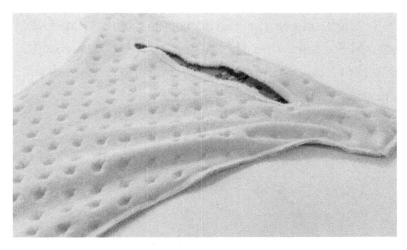

Cloth diaper sewed right sides together.

Step 6: Turn the diaper right-side out through your pocket. Make sure to poke the corners out so the diaper lays flat.

Step 7: Top stitch.

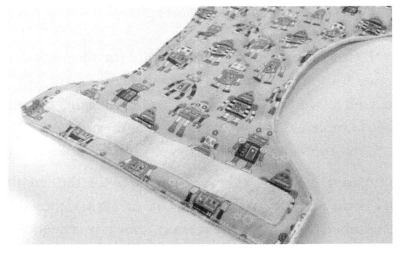

Top stitched cloth diaper.

Step 8: Mark where the elastic casings will go and sew the casing. Make sure that the casing is the correct width for your elastic. Backstitch at the beginning and end of your casing to make sure that area is secure.

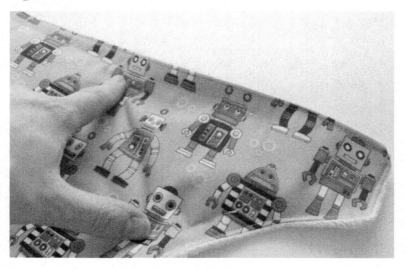

Casings for the back and leg elastics.

Step 9: Cut three pieces of elastic: one for the back casing and two for the leg casings. To determine the sizes, you can hold your elastic over the casing and pull taut, but don't pull it completely taut. That's the length you need. Make sure to cut the same exact length for both leg holes.

Some people use the following equation for the length of their elastic: add 1 in to the length of the casing, then divide that number by two. This equation does a pretty good job at estimating the correct length, although I add a tiny bit so I have extra on either side of where I tack down the elastic. This allows me to seam rip the area I tacked down and loosen the elastic if needed later (my babies have chunky legs!).

Attach a safety pin to the elastic and feed it through the casing. Tack down the end of the elastic on one side and sew over it.

Finish pulling the elastic all the way through. Once it's all the way through and has the proper tightness, sew down the other end. Be sure not to hit the safety pin. Remove the safety pin. Do the same for the other elastic cuts and casings.

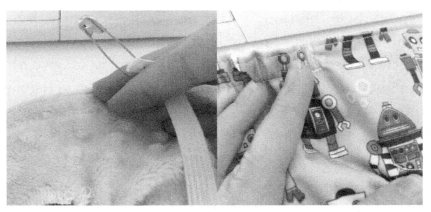

Left, a safety pin helps you pull elastic through a casing; right, the elastic sewn down at the end of the back and leg casings.

Step 10: Sew the hook tabs on. Mine hang off my diaper partially. I used a zig-zag stitch to attach them and went over quite a few times because this part of the diaper takes a lot of wear and tear.

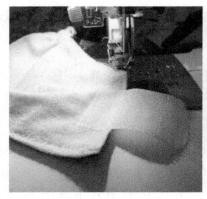 

Left, sewing the hook tabs on. Right, using a zig-zag stitch to attach the hook tabs to the diaper.

Step 11: Sew the laundry tabs on. This is optional, but I think it's necessary to improve the longevity of your diapers. The purpose of the laundry tabs is to give you something to hook onto when the diaper is open and going through the wash. Otherwise the hook gets hair, fuzz, other fabrics, and more stuck to it.

Left, laundry tabs sewn on. Right, closed laundry tabs with no hook exposed when closed.

Here are the finished products:

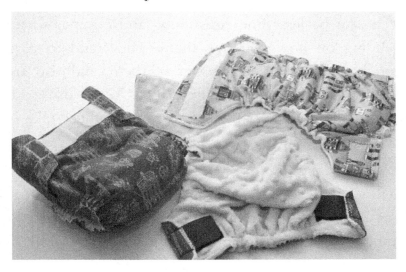

Completed extra-large diapers.

Side view.

How to Sew a Cloth Diaper Cover

Covers can be less time consuming and cheaper to make depending on how you sew them. They tend to require fewer materials, you need fewer of them, and you aren't sewing a stay-dry layer or absorbency. You'll use a fitted diaper or prefold under the cover. Both of those take time to sew, but prefolds are fairly inexpensive to buy, so I like that option.

I don't generally make one-size covers; I find that it's easier to make sized covers. They only require one layer of PUL in most cases (no interior fabric), and some fold over elastic around the edges. You can add snaps or hook and loop for the closure. Sewing them this way makes it much faster to whip out five or six at a time, which is my goal for making newborn diapers. I don't want to invest a lot of time in a diaper that won't be worn for very long.

The only difficult thing about sewing these is learning how to sew the fold-over elastic. It's similar to adding bias tape in that the fold-over elastic is folded over the fabric edges. You use a three-step zig-zag stitch to sew it on. The tricky part is stretching the elastic along the legs and back. I always wish I had an extra hand or two to make this easier. Let's get started.

HOW TO SEW, USE, AND CLEAN CLOTH DIAPERS

Step-by-Step Instructions

Step 1: Cut the PUL.

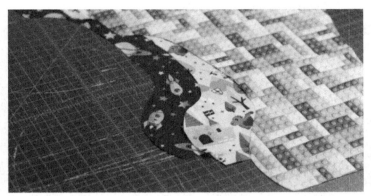

PUL cut out for three newborn covers.

Step 2: Sew the hook and loop on for the closure or add snaps. Add the snap-down rise if applicable. I'm using a newborn pattern that has a snap-down to lower the rise for the umbilical cord (so it doesn't rub the cord).

Make sure to reinforce the snaps with scrap PUL. The photo below shows the reinforced snaps on the inside of the Lego-themed diaper.

Loop sewn onto the front of a diaper cover. Snaps to adjust rise below.

Step 3: Mark where the back and leg elastics start and stop on the inside of the diaper. In the photo below, I used tailor's chalk to make my marks.

White marks at the legs and back where the elastic needs to be stretched.

Step 4: Fold the elastic over the edges of the diaper cut and use a wide three-step zig-zag stitch to sew it on. You'll sew it on normally, similar to bias tape, when you are sewing around most portions of the diaper. Make sure the zig-zag goes over the inner edge of the fold-over elastic or it will curl up.

When you get to the markings for the leg and back elastic, stretch the fold-over elastic tight as you sew. This is easier said than done, but you will get the hang of it as you go.

One trick is to sew the fold-over elastic on normally until the beginning mark for the stretch around the leg or back, find where the unstretched elastic will touch the next mark, then mark the halfway point on your elastic. That mark is where the elastic should touch the end mark for the stretch to the elastic. With my right hand, I grasp the mark on my elastic and hold it over the mark on my diaper. With my left hand, I grasp and hold the elastic and diaper on the other side of the needle (so it won't bend the needle). Then I can pull with my right hand so the elastic is stretched out and use a finger to push the PUL into the elastic fold. I sew as I hold it all taunt.

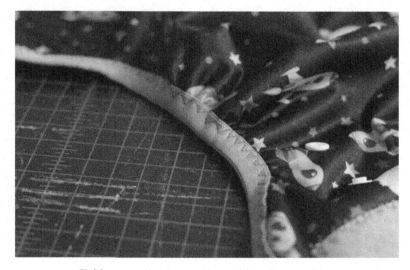

Folder-over elastic sewed on with a zig-zag stitch.
Using a three step zig-zag is preferred.

Step 5: Finish by adding the tabs that will close the diaper. If you're using snaps, don't forget to reinforce the snaps with scrap PUL.

Completed newborn diaper cover.

Here are some finished photos.

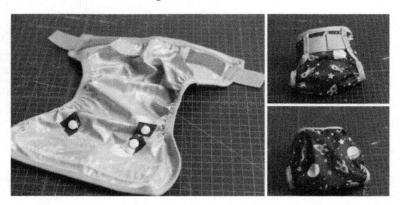

Left, newborn diaper cover, open interior; right, front and back of the closed cover.

How to Sew a Cloth Diaper Insert

There are a lot of ways to sew inserts. This makes it a bit tricky to explain how to make one, although they're quite simple to make. Many people just fold up prefolds to use as inserts in their pocket diapers. These work well and have great absorbency. Others sew a "snake" style insert that is long and folds over onto itself one or more times. The benefit to the snake style is that it unfolds for washing and drying, making it quicker to dry.

I prefer a standard-length insert with moderate thickness, but I sometimes use an extra insert if needed to add absorbency for a heavy wetter.

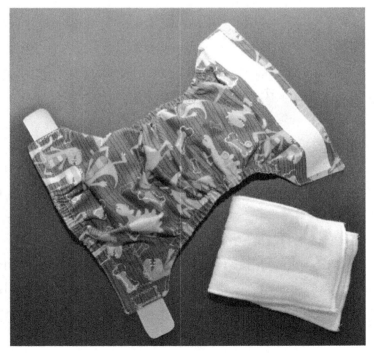

A diaper with handmade insert.

When I first started sewing cloth diapers, I would purchase three-layer bamboo inserts in bulk from a large retailer, then sew two of them together at the top. This would allow them to dry faster because they weren't attached the whole way around. Prices went up, however, so I wouldn't necessarily suggest that as the most affordable option.

Making inserts is fairly simple with a serger, some time, and patience.

Fabric Options for Inserts

Start by deciding on what type of fabric you want to make your inserts out of. Some people mix and match fabrics because different fabrics have different benefits. Some absorb faster, some absorb more, some can be used against a baby's skin, and some can't touch a baby's skin. Some people prefer a more organic option. Mixing and match allows you to get the best of all worlds, but I like to keep it simple.

Microfiber, one of the first and most popular choices for inserts, can cause rashes for some babies if it's placed against the skin. While I generally use pocket diapers where there's a layer of stay-dry fabric between the baby's bottom and the insert, I don't use microfiber because I like the flexibility of being able to use my inserts in an AI2 diaper where the insert is against the skin. Also, my husband struggles to keep track of which inserts are which, so it's just easier to simplify diaper changes.

I purchase all of my absorbency fabric from a cloth diaper

sewing website rather than going to a store and trying to figure out which fabrics are absorbent enough. By reading reviews on each fabric and the product description, I can make an educated choice on the best option for my diaper and baby. I have also found that local stores have limited options for absorbency fabric.

There's a trade off with fabrics: If your fabric holds a lot of liquid and is thinner, then you'll likely find it also takes longer to dry and is heavier. If it doesn't hold a lot of liquid, then you're using more layers and you may have a thicker but lightweight insert.

- Microfiber: You can upcycle microfiber towels or purchase microfiber fabric to sew your inserts. Many people use microfiber and sandwich it between bum-friendly fabrics. Or they use microfiber-only inserts in pocket diapers.
- Terry cloth: Old towels work as absorbency for inserts as well. The number of layers you use will depend on the thickness of your towels. If you're using old towels, you may need to strip them to make them absorbent again.
- Flannel: You can sew layers of heavy cotton flannel together for absorbency. This is a great way to upcycle old flannel sheets or blankets.
- Hemp: Hemp is a popular fabric that can absorb quite a bit of liquid, but it is slow to absorb. Usually it's used behind another insert with quicker absorbency or in combination with a quicker-

absorbing fabric. The hemp part of the insert would be furthest from the baby's skin.

- Bamboo: This has been my preferred option because it is soft, it softens more with each wash, and it is safe against the skin. The company I purchase my fabric from offers a super heavy bamboo fleece that works for a 2–3-layer insert.
- Cotton: Cotton Sherpa, cotton fleece, and cotton French terry are good options for inserts. I find that the cotton options are less expensive per yard than bamboo, hemp, or microfiber.

How Many Layers Do I Use?

This depends largely on the type of fabric you use and whether your baby is a heavy wetter. The main thing to keep in mind is that you don't want your inserts to be too thick because they will take a *very* long time to dry. This is particularly true if you plan to line dry your diapers and inserts.

Your best option is to use multiple thinner inserts instead of one super thick insert. If you have a heavy wetter, I'd suggest making some nice hemp inserts to use behind your normal insert to add absorbency without adding thickness.

A newborn diaper doesn't need to have as many layers because newborns need more diaper changes and produce less urine (smaller bladders). Newborn inserts are also shorter because the diaper is shorter.

Step-by-Step Instructions

Step 1: Absorbent fabrics shrink in the wash, so you either need to account for shrinkage when you cut your fabric or you need to prewash. Some fabrics are easier to sew before washing, so keep that in mind.

Step 2: Decide how many layers you want per insert and cut all of the fabric for your inserts. My insert is three layers thick. It is 13.5 in long and 5.5 in wide, fitting inside the one-size diapers well.

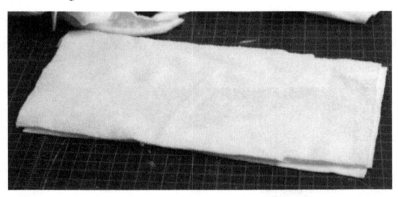

Three layers of fabric cut for a diaper insert.

Step 3: Pin insert fabrics together.

Step 4: Sew a straight stitch up the middle of your insert. I like to do this when I'm using more than two layers of fabric because it helps hold the fabric in place as I serge.

Straight stitch up the center of an insert.

Step 5: Serge around your insert, making sure to catch all of the layers. I like rounded corners on inserts because I think they're faster to sew.

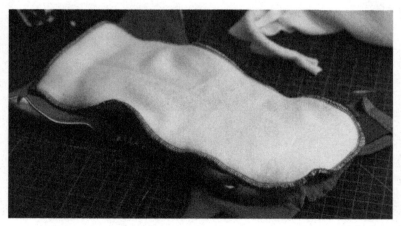

Serged rounded edges for a diaper insert.

Once you've completed the insert, you can insert it into your pocket diaper.

Insert inside a pocket diaper.

Adding Custom Touches to Cloth Diapers: Ruffles and More

The sky is the limit when customizing cloth diapers. People do some creative things to customize their diapers, and due to the expensive materials involved and the time it takes to make them, these diapers can be pricey. I love to stalk the special custom sales to see how much the diapers sell for—it's fun to see people spend $200 for a diaper. I have to wonder if the diapers go on display or actually get worn.

The nice thing about sewing your own diapers is that you can customize them yourself. Just keep in mind that many of the customized diapers are worth their hefty price tag because of how time intensive they are to make.

Convenience, clothing, and accessibility are important things to remember when you customize a diaper. If you add some types of fabric to the diaper, you might find yourself unable to wash it diaper in a hot wash cycle. If you add a tail and it isn't removable, you won't be able to put clothing on over the diaper. These are details you want to consider.

Here are some possible custom touches to add to your diapers:

Patchwork Diapers

This is one the simplest and least difficult diapers to pull off. I love to save my scrap PUL and make patchwork diapers. They're adorable. I've used scraps to make patriotic diapers or just to throw together some of my favorite fabrics. While it can be time consuming, it's still feasible. The nice thing about the patchwork diapers is that it's still possible to put a pair of pants on over them. There's no difference in how they wear.

The big difference in sewing them is that you are creating a lot of extra holes in the PUL, which may make it prone to leaking. As such, you need to line the inside with an additional layer of PUL (plain PUL is cheaper and therefore a good option since it won't show). This only applies to PUL diapers, however. Some people will make fitted diapers in patchwork, and in that case, you'll put a diaper cover over it to contain leaks.

This was during the process for creating a patriotic diaper...

Pieces for a striped American flag diaper.

This is the finished product:

Patriotic Diaper

Ruffles

I have two little boys with a third on the way, which means I haven't really had many opportunities to make girly diapers. I have, however, created some ruffle-butt diapers for friends with little girls because I can't help myself and need to live vicariously through others.

One of the things to be aware of is that the ruffle can make it difficult to slip a pair of pants on. Some people make their ruffles removable and some do not. Many cloth-diapering parents just use these customized diapers for nice days when they're letting their child play at home without pants. We have a lot of those days because cloth diapering parents like to show off our cute cloth diapers. It comes with the territory. And nobody likes to show off as much as a parent who *made* the diapers herself.

Ruffle-butt diapers are made by sewing a ruffle with coordinating fabric, making sure to finish any raw edges that could fray. You can add a couple of snaps to the ruffle, then add the coordinating snaps to where you want the ruffle placed on the diaper (don't forget to reinforce your snaps). Then the ruffle just snaps on. Alternatively, you could sew the ruffle directly on to the back of the diaper. Generally ruffles are placed on the back of the diaper.

Below is a ruffle-butt diaper I made for a friend.

Ruffle-butt diaper with a removable ruffle.

Flowers, Tails, and Fins

These have the same potential problems as the ruffle-butt diapers in that it can be hard to slip pants on over the accessories. I make the accessories removable to solve this problem. Please keep in mind any safety issues with additions; you don't want to add choking hazards to your diaper unless you plan to closely supervise. You'll also want to consider how you'll launder the accessories—if you can't launder them, make sure they're easily removable.

I added little removable handmade flowers to this one. The ruffles are sewn on. The button hides the snap underneath.

Snap-on flowers for the back of a diaper.

People get creative with additions to the backs of cloth diapers. Dinosaur tails, bunny tails, and mermaid fins are favorites! I recommend searching the internet for "dinosaur tail cloth diapers." You won't be disappointed. Those huge additions really need to be removable though.

Applique Diapers

I've seen some applique cloth diapers sell for a lot of money, and justifiably so. The person making them put in a lot of work to create a custom design, and the seller usually auctions the diaper off. Search "Baa Baa Baby Yoshi Diaper" if you want to see what a $200 diaper looks like. It's stunning. Fitted diapers are probably the best option for applique diapers because PUL would not be waterproof after that much sewing on it.

Embroidered Diapers

Embroidered diapers are nice if you have an embroidery machine that you know how to use. You can add monograms, cute designs, or whatever your heart desires. You have three options for embroidering diapers, keeping in mind that you need your diaper to be water resistant.

The first option is to embroider a cotton exterior, then do a hidden PUL interior. This can be a bit more complicated because the cotton exterior, if done incorrectly, can wick moisture from the inside of the diaper onto the exterior. There are ways to make it work, but overall I don't recommend it. There are two reasons I don't like this combo: First, PUL has a stretch to it and cotton does not. I don't like the combination. Second, I don't think the cotton has the ability to stand up to wear and tear as well as PUL does.

Back when PUL design options were limited, we would use a work around to make cotton exteriors so we could have pretty diapers. Now there are so many fantastic PUL design options that you really don't need to go to these extremes. But I want to mention the option because it does exist and there are tutorials to explain how to do it if you have a cotton print that you just *must* have.

A second option is to embroider the exterior fabric of a fitted diaper. Your cover will go over it when you're out, but your baby can easily wear the fitted diaper by itself around the house. You'll just need to change it immediately when you see it's wet. This is a pretty easy option.

The third option is to embroider the PUL exterior. This is touchy because the more holes you put in PUL, the greater the chance that the diaper will leak. It can, however, be done successfully. I've made two embroidered diapers and neither leaked.

If you want to try embroidering, this blog post is a great resource. I've done it this way and the diapers didn't leak, but I don't want to butcher a tutorial on the process as I'm not a fan of embroidery and it has been a while since I made mine. Here are some photos of my embroidery process, however.

First I embroidered a dinosaur through the exterior PUL, a large scrap piece of PUL, and a piece of stabilizer. Once the embroidery is done, the scrap fabric is folded over and sewn up, enclosing it all. Excess fabric from the scrap is trimmed away.

Here is one of the finished embroidered diapers I made.

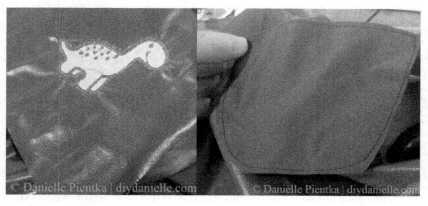

Left, embroidery on a cloth diaper. Right, Closure over the embroidered PUL to prevent leaks.

Embroidered cloth diaper.

Options for Sewing Cloth Diapers on a Budget

Many choose to cloth diaper to save money; as such, they may not have a lot to spend to start their stash. I think a lot of people decide to sew their own diapers in hopes that it will save them even more money—and it will, to a point.

Before I explain some ways to save money, keep in mind that if you don't have access to a sewing machine, then I recommend buying cloth diapers new (or used) to save money. Buying a machine and the supplies necessary to sew cloth diapers will make any money you save negligible. If you already own or can borrow a machine and supplies, it is possible to save money by sewing cloth diapers

Choose the Right Fabric

I tend to buy the more expensive prints, so my price per diaper is higher than it needs to be. My diaper supplies tend to run about $10 per diaper, and because I use quality products, I know they'll last. I can also resell the diapers when I'm done with them. Most store diapers run $20–25 per diaper, so sewing my own does save money.

You can save money by buying solid PUL instead. You may also be able to save money if you find someone trying to sell leftover PUL from their own projects. PUL is sold by the yard, but if you can purchase multiple continuous yards, you'll be able to get more diaper cuts from it all. There's a lot of math involved, but sewing 20 diapers from several yards of plain PUL is cheaper than buying enough designer PUL in 22-in cuts for 20 different diapers.

If you opt to purchase PUL with a design printed on it, keep in mind that how the print is designed can affect how many diaper cuts you'll get from each yard. You'll always want the stretch of your fabric across the waistband of the diaper, so you can't place your diaper pattern horizontally across your PUL to cut it. You can, however, fit more cuts on a width of PUL by flipping your pattern vertically. This only works if your fabric is solid or the pattern is bidirectional (e.g., if a design element is facing both up and down).

Tip: Usually you'll want the design to be the correct side up on the butt of the diaper because that's the portion of the diaper you'll see the most of when your one-year-old runs away from you to get in to trouble. Also, the print on the front is frequently obscured by the hook and loop or snaps.

Choose the Right Style

To further save money on sewing cloth diapers, I recommend skipping pocket, AIO, or AI2 diapers completely. They are more expensive, more complicated, and more time consuming to sew. They are also not the thriftiest option. Those fancy diapers are amazing and easy to use, but if you really need to save money, I recommend using covers with a prefold or a fitted diaper underneath.

Prefolds are cheap to buy and cheap to make. You need a lot of them, but if your baby is just wet then you can swap out the prefold and reuse the cover. This means you need fewer covers, which is ideal when you're trying to save money. When you do need to wash them, covers also launder fairly quickly. You could easily hand wash and line dry them because they don't have thick fabric that needs to be cleaned.

Old wool sweaters can be upcycled to make covers as an alternative to PUL, and many people make prefolds or fitted diapers from upcycled fabrics. Old towels, t-shirts, and flannel blankets can all be used to sew these items. You just need to make sure that the fabric you use is absorbent. It's a great way to make use of old items, and you can even check your local freecycle or yard sale group to see if anyone has old clothing or linens that they would like to donate. Clothing that isn't in good enough condition to sell at a thrift or consignment store can still be upcycled into cloth diaper inserts, prefolds, or fitteds.

Prefolds are the easiest to sew because they're a simple rectangle and don't need elastic or any complicated sewing techniques. If you have a serger, it is quick and easy to make them by layering multiple rectangles of absorbent fabric, pinning them together, and serging around the edges. Otherwise, you can sew right sides together, leaving an area to turn them, and then turn, press, and top stitch.

I really like making fitted diapers from old t-shirts. They're cute and it's fun to play with the designs. This is a diaper that I made from an old shirt of mine. It was a great way to practice sewing cloth diapers before I tried making them with PUL.

Fitted diaper from an upcycled t-shirt.

Common Mistakes When Sewing Cloth Diapers

Stretch in Wrong Direction

Make sure the stretch goes across the waistline of the diaper. This applies to both your interior and exterior fabrics. I've made a few diapers with the stretch in the incorrect direction. They work for a while, but they don't have quite as long of a life span as diapers made correctly because the waistband doesn't stretch with your baby's tummy as he or she grows.

Leaving the Safety Pin Inside the Diaper

When you feed the elastic through the casings, make sure to remove the safety pin after. Also make sure you don't hit the safety pin when you're sewing the elastic down.

Cutting PUL in the Wrong Direction

In most cases, the butt of the diaper should show your fabric's print right-side up. The front of the diaper is generally obscured by snaps or hook and loop, so it doesn't matter as much if the fabric is upside down on that side. If you have a fabric that only goes in one direction, it will be wrong-side up on one side. Make sure it's the side you want it on!

Cutting the Elastic Too Short

You don't want the elastic to be too short; I always leave a little extra elastic on both ends of my casing so that I can go back and loosen it if needed. If you want to loosen the elastic but it is too short, you'd need to replace it completely.

Using the Wrong Thread or Needle

Always use the right size and type of needles and thread. It can make a difference in whether or not your diapers leak.

Using the Correct Snaps

Most people prefer to use female snaps on the front of their diapers, stating that male snaps may press into the baby's belly and be uncomfortable if the baby is laying on his or her stomach. I'm not sure how true this is given how much padding diapers have via the insert, but it's something to consider.

Using Poor-Quality Materials

I can't stress the importance of buying good materials for cloth diapers. While upcycling is amazing and I advocate strongly for doing so, items like elastic and hook and loop should be brand new. They should also be *made for diapers*. I've had poor-quality hook and loop fray and stop holding. It's awful and is not easy to fix after you've finished sewing the diaper. The name-brand hook and loop that you may be familiar with is *not* made for the amount of wear, tear, and washing that diapers sustain.

Repairing Cloth Diapers

I don't have a lot of experience repairing cloth diapers, but once you understand how to make them, repairing them is usually not a difficult process. It can, however, be time consuming, so you need to decide if you'd rather sell or give them away, disclosing that they need to repairs, or if you want to tackle the task of repairing them yourself. They sell for less if they need repairs, so repairing them is beneficial.

The one thing that you really can't repair is the fabric. Ripped, worn PUL will leak. There may be ways to patch it, but it may not be worth it. I have a couple of diapers that I accidentally cut when I was making them, and I used a good glue to cover the spot; it worked, but it's not pretty.

Snaps usually are pretty sturdy, although occasionally I put one on incorrectly and need to replace it. In that case, I remove the snap and put a new snap in the old hole.

The two main things that usually need replacing and that are worth replacing are elastic and hook and loop. Elastic wears out over time; I think the urine and wash cycles tend to break it down faster. It gets stiff and crackles, and if you wait long enough, it may even snap.

Hook and loop gets worn out and can stop sticking together as well. Hook in particular can get pieces of fabric and other yucky things stuck in it.

Upgrades for Used Diapers

If you buy used cloth diapers, here are three adjustments you may want to make to them:

1. Add a Laundry Tab

If your diaper didn't come with a laundry tab, I highly recommend sewing one on. You just sew it right next to your tab with a zig-zag stitch—similar to how it's done in the diaper sewing tutorial—so you can fold the tab closed when the diaper goes through the wash. This will extend the life of your hook and loop.

Laundry tabs on a cloth pocket diaper.

2. Replace the Elastic

The ease of this process depends on the diaper and how the elastic was installed to begin with.

Adjustable elastic: If the elastic is adjustable, you may find that it can be easily pulled out and replaced without any sewing at all. You'll just need to find the replacement elastic with the holes in it for adjusting the size.

Elastic in a casing: If the elastic has a casing and is sewn down at either end of the casing, it's fairly easy to replace. The following is a tutorial for how to replace elastic in a casing; you'll need a seam ripper, a sewing machine (or you can hand stitch), a safety pin or bodkin, polyester thread, and new diaper elastic. Before getting started, you must also measure how wide the casing is to make sure the new elastic is the right width.

Step 1: The old elastic will be sewn down on each end of the casing. You need to seam rip *only the thread that holds down the elastic* to release the elastic. Do not seam rip the sides of the casing.

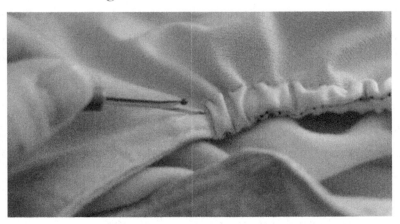

Seam ripping the thread that was holding the elastic down in the casing.

Step 2: Remove the old elastic and throw it away.

Step 3: Measure and replace the elastic as outlined in my

diaper sewing tutorial for the pocket diaper. It's the same process.

Step 4: Repeat for all other elastics. Cloth diapers should have a back elastic and an elastic for each leg area. I would replace them all at once, even if some seem like they're in better condition.

Note: If the elastic was zig-zag stitched down for the entire length, it's a much more difficult process. I am not going to cover that because it will depend on the diaper and how it was designed. I recommend checking YouTube for a tutorial if you have a name-brand diaper you'd like to replace the elastics on.

3. Replace the Hook and Loop

Removing the hook for the tabs is pretty easy. You need a seam ripper, some quality replacement hook in the correct color, and a sewing machine. First, carefully use the seam ripper to cut the stitching that holds the hook on the diaper, removing the hook when finished. Make sure to remove any extra pieces of thread. Next, use your sewing machine with a zig-zag stitch to sew the new piece of hook on as a tab. You can use the old hook as a template for size.

Replacing the loop along the front of the diaper could be more complicated depending on what type of diaper it is. If it's a cover and sewn like the new ones in my tutorial, you can just seam rip the loop, remove it, and sew on the new loop.

For pocket diapers, however, you must seam rip the top of

the diaper above the loop. This opens up the top of the diaper, giving you access to just the loop and PUL. You won't touch the interior fabric. You can seam rip your loop (cut the threads holding it on to the diaper), remove it and all the extra loose thread, and replace it with new loop. Make sure the loop covers the entire area the old loop did. Zig-zag stitch the loop on to the diaper. Then you can top stitch your diaper closed along the top front where you seam ripped.

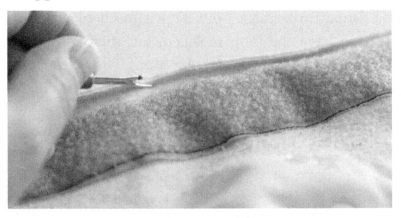

Seam ripping the top stitching on the front of a diaper before replacing the loop.

Selling Used Cloth Diapers

Used diapers have great resale value. If you do a good job sewing your cloth diapers and care for them properly, it's reasonable to expect to sell your used diapers for up to $5–15 per diaper. The resale value makes cloth diapers reasonable for many families.

If you're considering selling used diapers, keep in mind that certain factors will impact how much you can sell them for:

- Sewing quality
- Current condition (stains, wear, and tear)
- The condition of the elastic, hook and loop, or snaps
- The pattern on the diaper (some patterns will be more sought after)

You can increase how much you get for your cloth diapers by replacing elastic or hook and loop that is not in good condition.

Some damage may make your diaper unsellable. The diaper below can have the loop replaced, but there is damage to the front of the PUL below the loop. The diaper doesn't leak, but the interior and exterior are not in great condition. I would give this away, not attempt to sell it.

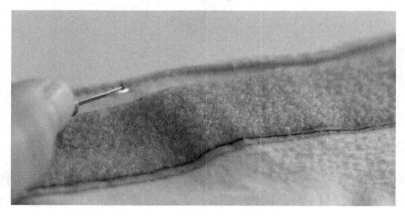

Damage to the front of a cloth diaper lowers resale value.

7 SEWING OTHER REUSABLE CLOTH PRODUCTS

How to Sew Cloth Wipes, Family Cloth, Unpaper Towels, & Cloth Napkins

These are all made using the same method. There are various options for fabric choices, but I love using flannel fabric. It's affordable if I buy it on sale, it absorbs well, and there are cute designs. For napkins and cloth wipes, there are so many cute children's fabrics, but I can also find nice fabrics for adults, too.

When we first started cloth diapering, we bought some cloth wipes that had a soft fabric on the back. I struggle with these because they don't absorb water as easily.

I make my wipes two-ply (two sided). Accordingly, I cut two squares for each wipe (see sizes below) and serge them together with the right sides out.

Sizes for Fabric Cuts

- Cloth wipes/family cloth: 8 in by 8 in
- Unpaper towels: 10 in by 10 in
- Cloth napkins: 6 in by 6 in

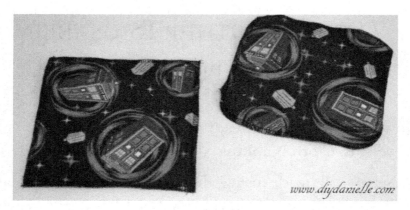

Serged cloth napkins. Square corners vs. rounded corners.

A note on sizes: You can play with the sizes and make them the size that works best for you. Figuring out how you plan to store them will help you decide the perfect size to fit your storage space. Making them different sizes can also help you sort them when you're putting away clean laundry.

A note about serging: If you don't have a serger, you can sew the two pieces right sides together—leaving a small opening—and turn right-side out to topstitch the opening closed. Alternatively, you can face them wrong sides together and zig-zag stitch around them to finish the edges and prevent fraying.

Would you prefer to see a video about how to make these items? Check out my YouTube video, How to Serge Cloth Wipes, Unpaper Towels, Family Cloth, Cloth Napkins, etc.

How to Sew Nursing Pads

Nursing pads made with a sewing machine.

I make my nursing pads with PUL fabric for the exterior, several layers of absorbency fabric in the middle, and Alova Suedecloth on the interior (next to the breast). The suedecloth helps wick any moisture into the absorbency, while the PUL keeps the moisture from leaking through to your clothing. You can also experiment with other wicking fabrics for the interior.

For a pattern, I've found that an old CD—yes, a compact disc—works well. It's a lot easier to use than a paper pattern because you can lay it on the fabric, zip around the CD with a rotary cutter, and easily cut out the layers.

To sew nursing pads, you'll need one layer of PUL, one layer of a wicking fabric, and some layers of absorbency fabric. I have used upcycled t-shirts and needed several layers to make enough absorbency, but I also use scraps of bamboo fabric and other new fabrics from sewing diaper inserts; those require fewer layers. Flannel would also work for absorbency. The number of interior layers you need depends on how much absorbency the fabric has. Don't forget to cut enough for the correct number of pairs.

You will layer your fabrics exactly as you want them for the nursing pads—right sides out. Pin each pad together. Sew around the circle with straight and zig-zag stitches. If you have a serger, you can serge around the circle.

Here is the finished product:

Nursing pads finished with a serger.

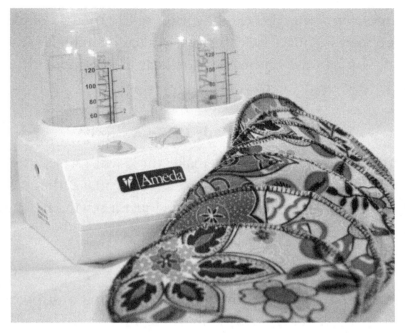

Completed nursing pads made with a sewing machine and zig-zag stitch.

How to Sew Handkerchiefs

I won't get very detailed about how to sew these because they aren't complicated. If you don't own a serger, just go buy some already made handkerchiefs. It will be cheaper and easier. Or find a non-fraying fabric to use and just cut your squares.

If you own a serger, find a nice, soft fabric that you won't mind blowing your nose on, and serge around one cut of it. Mine are all one ply. I made a bunch of smaller-sized handkerchiefs, but I think large ones work better if you want to get multiple uses out of one.

For fabric type, I think one layer of flannel would be the

cheapest option if you can buy it on sale. I tried a couple of other fabrics, but I love flannel for handkerchiefs. If you want, you can use embroidery or heat transfer vinyl to add decorative elements to your handkerchiefs.

How to Sew Menstrual Pads (Mama Cloth)

I'm going to cover how to make these with a serger and sewing machine combined. I've tried to make them with the turn and topstitch method using just a sewing machine, but they're very bulky that way.

Materials

- Pattern—you can make a pattern using a disposable pad, or there are free mama cloth patterns available online.
- Larger pieces with wings: One cut of bubble minky fabric and one cut of a coordinating fabric. The coordinating fabric should be a type that won't slip around on your underwear.
- Smaller pieces without wings: One piece of PUL, shiny side up; two layers of bamboo double loop terry fabric; and one layer of bubble minky with the right side of the fabric up.
- Sewing machine and serger

Altogether I had six layers of fabric per pad. You may need more or less absorbency, depending on how heavy your period is and when you want to use these during your period.

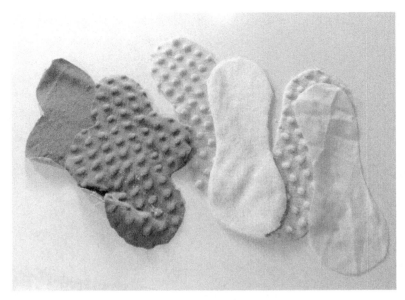

Cuts of fabric for sewing cloth menstrual pads.

Step-by-Step Instructions

Step 1: Pin and serge the two pieces with wings together right-side out. Make sure to turn off the knife for this step; if you leave it on, it's really hard to get around the curves without making the fabric look like a crime scene.

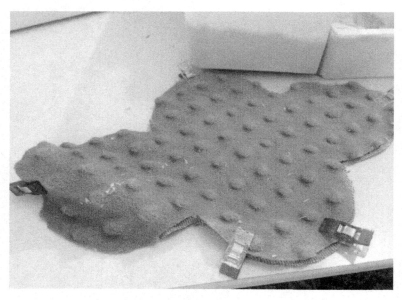
Layers for cloth menstrual pads pinned together.

Step 2: Serge around all of the pieces without wings in the following order: one piece of PUL, shiny side up; two layers of bamboo double loop terry fabric; and one layer of bubble minky with the right side of the fabric up.

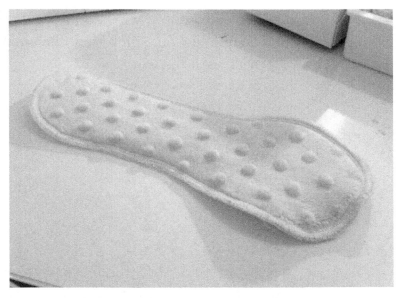

Smaller cuts of fabric serged together.

Here are the two sections side by side:

All of the pieces ready to complete a cloth menstrual pad.

Step 3: Lay the smaller piece without wings onto the fabric with wings and pin. Using a zig-zag stitch, sew the smaller piece onto the larger piece with the wings.

Sewing the smaller piece on to the winged piece.

Step 4: Add snaps to the wings. One snap faces up; the other, down.

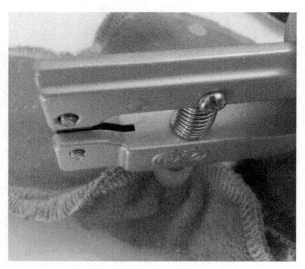

Adding snaps to the wings on mama cloth.

Your menstrual pad is now finished. You can even fold it smaller for easy storage. To do so, fold in one end, fold in the other end over that, then snap the wings closed.

Mama cloth, folded for easy storage.

Completed cloth menstrual pad, open.

Here's an image of the bottom of the mama cloth while snapped. The snapped wings would go around your underwear, similar to a disposable pad.

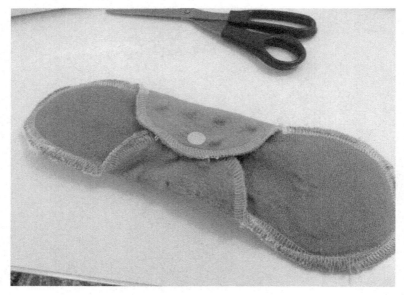

Bottom of the cloth menstrual pad.

How to Sew Wet Bags

You can make wet bags with a cotton exterior and a PUL interior, but I adore having one cute PUL fabric for the entire wet bag. It also makes the process a lot faster and easier.

Size is a matter of personal preference. You just need an opening wide enough to fit your dirty items through. Smaller bags are great for heading to the pool or for on the go. I use a medium wet bag in our bathroom for cloth menstrual pads and family cloth, but I hang large wet bags in our bathrooms for dirty diapers.

Fabric Cuts for a Medium Wet Bag

- Strap: 16 in by 3.5 in
- Large cut of PUL fabric: 29.5 in by 16 in (You will fold this piece in half so the fold is along the bottom of the bag. Make sure the fabric, if directional, goes in the correct direction.)
- Zipper: 21 in (I could have used a shorter zipper if I'd had one)

Step-by-Step Instructions

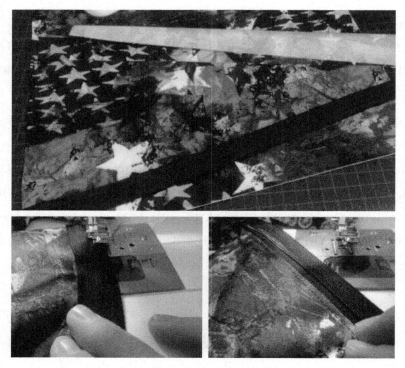

Sewing a zipper on a wet bag.

Step 1: Once you've cut your fabric pieces, lay the zipper face down onto the right side of your fabric along where you want the mouth of the bag to be. Using a zipper foot, sew the zipper on and top stitch.

Step 2: Now sew the other side of the zipper on to the other side of the wet bag mouth. To do so, fold the wet bag in half with the zipper face down on the other right side of the wet bag's mouth. Sew with your zipper foot. You'll need to flip the bag in an odd way to topstitch the zipper on this side.

Step 3: Sew the strap. Fold the strap fabric in half, right sides together, and sew along two sides. Turn the strap right-side out and topstitch three sides.

Step 4: Once finished topstitching, pin the bag right sides together. Open the zipper enough so you'll be able to turn the bag right-side out when you're done. I used clips rather than pins to avoid putting extra holes in my PUL. Sandwich the strap between the fabric near the bag's mouth.

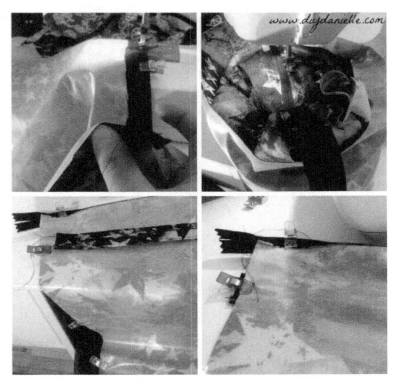

Top, sewing the zipper on the wet bag; bottom, sewing the wet bag sides.

Step 5: Sew along both sides to close the bag. I used my serger, but a regular sewing machine with a straight stitch will work fine. Use polyester thread for sewing PUL.

Top, serged sides on a wet bag; bottom, optional steps to create a boxy bottom.

Step 6 (optional): This step creates a boxy bottom, which isn't a necessary feature. If you are newer to sewing, it's easier to skip this step. Most of my wet bags have a flat bottom. This step is pictured in the two bottom images in the collage above.

For this step, put your thumb on the side seam and your palm under the bottom of the bag. Pinch. You'll sew across, creating a triangle. A bigger triangle will give your bag a larger boxy bottom. It will also make your bag shorter. I keep my triangles pretty small. Once you sew across, cut off the triangle end. I finished my edges with a serger to make them look more professional. You can zig-zag them if you don't own a serger or just skip this step.

Step 7: Turn your bag right-side out through the opening you left in the zipper. Add a male snap to the end of your strap and a female snap to the top of your strap. Some people use a closed loop, but a snapping loop allows you to snap it around something—for example, a towel bar. Hook and loop would work as an alternative to snaps, but I think that snaps are easier to deal with in the wash and that they hold weight better.

Snaps being added to the strap on a wet bag.

Finished wet bag.

How to Sew Refrigerator Liners

Refrigerator liners are very easy to make using PUL. I made two sets so I can swap them out for washing.

Materials

- Measuring tape
- PUL fabric
- Optional: Sewing machine or serger

Step 1: Measure your refrigerator's shelves (the glass part only, not the plastic edge) and add a small seam allowance. In my case, the shelf was 13.75 in by 14.75 in. I cut a piece of fabric that was 14.25 in by 15.25 in. If you have directional fabric, make sure the fabric is facing the right direction so your design is facing you when you open the refrigerator.

Step 2 (optional): Serge around the edges of the fabric to give it a finished look. If you don't have a serger, you can zig-zag the edges or skip finishing the edges. PUL does not fray so you could treat this as a no-sew project.

Step 3: Install. Wipe down the shelves with a damp sponge and do not dry. You want it to be a little moist so the PUL will "stick." Lay your PUL liner shiny side down on the glass shelf.

Completed shelf liner.

How to Sew Reusable Snack Bags

Materials

- PUL fabric
- Snaps, hook and loop, or zipper for a closure
- Sewing machine or serger

Step-by-Step Instructions

Step 1: Cut the fabric. The measurements for my fabric were 8.5 in by 16.5 in. It's only one cut because you'll fold the 16.5-in length in half.

Step 2: Cut the strap fabric; fold it right sides together and sew two of the sides. Then turn it right-side out. Top stitch, leaving the unfinished side.

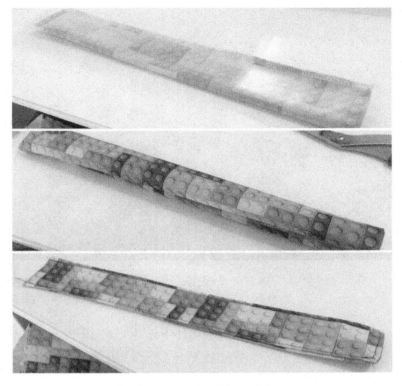

Sewing a strap for the snack bag.

Step 3: Cut the hook and loop to be slightly less than the width of the fabric. Sew it, using a zig-zag stitch, on to the right sides of each end of the fabric. The hook will be on one end and the loop on the other.

Hook and loop sewn on to the fabric for the reusable snack bag.

Step 4: Now fold the area with the hook and loop over (wrong sides together) and sew down. Then sew along the top edge. Repeat for the other side.

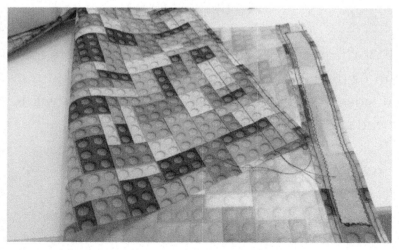

The hook and loop is now on the inside of the bag.

Step 5: Fold the fabric with the right sides together. Sandwich the raw edge of your strap along the top on one side. Pin and sew up along each side of the fabric.

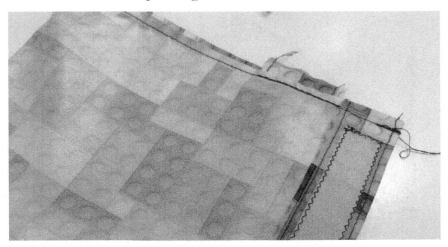

Sandwiched strap along the side of the snack bag. Sew with a straight stitch.

Step 6 *(optional, skip if you don't want boxy edges)*: Pinch the side seam with your thumb and the rest of your hand under the bottom of the bag. Then sew across the bottom in a triangle shape and cut off the bottom of the triangle. Do the same with the other side. When you turn your bag right-side out, your bag will have a nice boxy bottom.

Optional step to add a boxy bottom to bag.

Step 7: Add a snap or hook and loop to your strap.

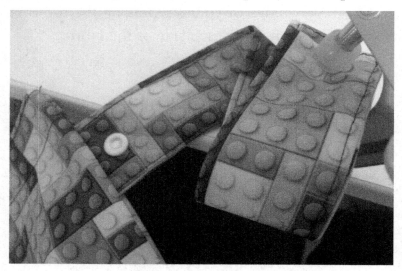

Snaps added to the strap.

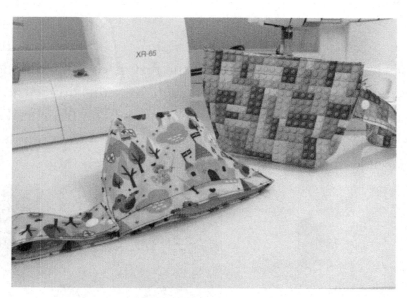

Completed reusable snack bags.

How to Sew Fabric Gift Bags

Materials

- Fabric: Cotton works fine for this. I love seasonal designs but also use scrap fabric from other projects.
- Sewing machine
- Ribbon or draw string
- Optional: eyelets

Fabric gift bags are very similar to any other type of drawstring bag. I only use one layer of fabric because a liner isn't really necessary unless your fabric is sheer or you need the extra padding to protect what is inside.

I made reusable gift bags in all different sizes, so I won't address the fabric sizes you'll need. This is up to you. If you have a rectangular cut of fabric that is big enough for a bag, just use that and you won't even need to cut your fabric.

Step-by-Step Instructions

1. Cut the fabric.

Fabric cut for a drawstring gift bag.

2. Fold the fabric with the right sides together and pin.

Fold right sides together and pin.

3. Sew along both sides. I used my serger. If you use a sewing machine and are using a fabric that frays, make sure to zig-zag the edges.

Sew along both sides of the bag.

4. As described in previous bag tutorials, I created a boxy edge on the bag's bottom.

Boxy bottom to the bag.

5. I serged around the top of the bag to finish the edges so they won't fray. No serger? Use a zig-zag stitch on your sewing machine instead.

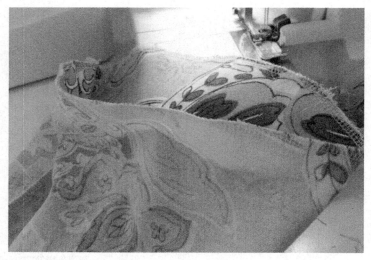

Serged top of the bag.

6. I decided where I wanted the drawstring to come out and marked the spot. Then I added eyelets. In the past, I've just made a button hole and used that. This is my first time using eyelets, so they aren't perfect.

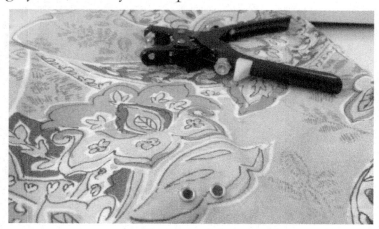

Eyelets added for the drawstring.

7. I folded over the edge of the bag, sewing around to close the casing.

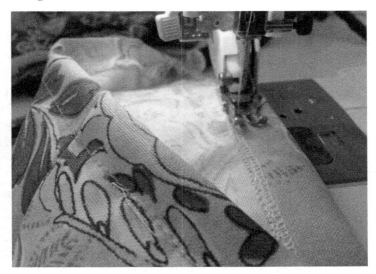

Using a straight stitch to create a casing on my bag.

8. Finally, I used a small safety pin to thread the drawstring (in this case, a ribbon) into an eyelet, through the entire casing, and out the other eyelet.

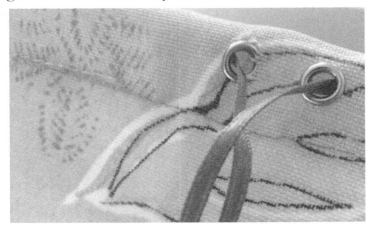

Ribbon used as a drawstring through the casing.

To label the bags, just include a card inside, pin on a tag, or add a chalkboard sticker to the exterior. You could also embroider a name on the bag or use heat-transfer vinyl.

Chalkboard label on the exterior of a fabric gift bag.

Here is the finished product:

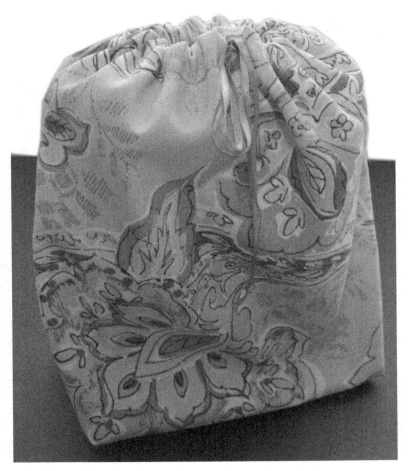

Finished reusable gift bag.

8 Make Your Own Cloth-Diaper-Friendly Diaper Rash Spray

Many diaper rash creams and sprays are not cloth-diaper friendly. They can cause repelling, which requires you to strip your diapers. It's a lot of extra work and isn't a gentle process, so many people use disposable diapers or liners when their child has diaper rash.

DIY Diaper Rash Spray

I have discovered that there are some reasonable options for making your own cloth-diaper-friendly creams. They are good for regular prevention, as well as minor rashes.

My favorite DIY recipe has been a diaper rash spray. It's easier to apply and doesn't require rubbing the cream into your child's skin. It uses tea tree essential oil, however, which is recommended for use after 6 months old. Please consult with your pediatrician before using essential oils on your child.

Materials

- Fractionated coconut oil
- Tea tree oil
- Spray bottle

Instructions

For every 1 oz of coconut oil you use to fill the bottle, add 1–2 drops of tea tree oil. Mix. Spray on your child's bottom as needed.

If you prefer to buy a cloth-diaper-friendly cream, you can find a few different brands online.

If you have to use a cream that isn't good for cloth diapers, use disposable diapers or a liner between your child's bottom and your cloth diapers to prevent repelling for the duration of the rash.

Conclusion

You made it to the end—congratulations! I know this is a lot to absorb, but don't stress. You don't need to do it all today or all at once. You don't even need to ever do it all. If there's a product or approach you love, start there. Any step you take toward being more environmentally friendly not only helps the environment, but it also saves you money.

What I love about cloth is that it's not all or nothing. When I first started using cloth products, I only used cloth diapers. I've slowly added more cloth products to our home, but I still haven't made enough handkerchiefs to say I've switched over completely. It's a work in progress. And over time, my cloth use has fluctuated. When my second son was born via c-section and my oldest was still in diapers, I didn't have the ability or resources to keep up with the laundry for both of them. I used a mix of disposable and cloth diapers—life happens.

We keep toilet paper, tissue, and paper towels for guests and special circumstances. I use disposable menstrual pads occasionally, particularly if I am going to be out for a while, if my cycle is really heavy, or if I'm traveling. We use disposable diapers for my youngest son when he is at preschool, and we also use them when we're on vacation.

Some people go all in: cloth or nothing. While it's admirable, I think it can be hard to do, and it takes significant lifestyle changes. I applaud the effort, but don't feel like you have to be there right now.

Over time, we've used fewer and fewer disposable items, and I've seen us save so much money. Every time we need to pick up disposable items, I'm reminded of the financial cost of using them, and I'm encouraged to continue on my journey with cloth.

I also love that we've reduced the amount of trash that we need to take out. My husband has it good because when we moved in together years ago, I said I'd do the laundry if he did the trash. This was before we transitioned to cloth. He lucked out because now I do all the laundry and he can get away with putting the trash out less frequently.

I hope my book has been helpful for you. If you have any questions or comments, please feel free to contact me at danielle@diydanielle.com.

If you visit my blog, I wrote a post, Easy Supply List for this eBook, that contains links to many products and supplies that I use. You can also subscribe to my blog, www.diydanielle.com, to get more ideas for reusable products and for other DIY tutorials.

Please consider leaving a review for my book on Amazon. Reviews are a huge help to me because they provide feedback and help increase exposure for my book on Amazon.

Links for Further Research

Baby registries: Amazon, Cottonbabies, and Target sell cloth diapers and have baby registries. However, I'm sure there are many others. You can also use a baby registry aggregator like Babylist to add links to any product from any website.

Cloth diaper rentals: Some online stores offer cloth diaper rentals so you can try out different options before making a purchase. You may find one diaper works better for you and your family. Here are just a few of your options for renting cloth diapers:

Jillian's Drawers Cloth Diaper Rental for Newborns

Modern Cloth Diapers Newborn Rental

Kissed by the Moon Cloth Diaper Rentals

ConsiderCloth.org: More information on cloth diapering and the benefits.

Detergent chart from The Diaper Jungle: Find safe detergents for cloth diapers.

Diaper Services: This is a list of diaper services registered with The Real Diaper Industry Association. Diaper services deliver fresh diapers to your door and take dirty ones to launder.

Diaper Sewing Instructions and Patterns from the blog Simple Diaper Sewing Tutorials. These are some of the best diaper patterns and instructions I've seen, and they're available for free. The author is absolutely wonderful to offer these detailed patterns, and she provides amazing, organized, and easy-to-follow tutorials.

Diaper Sewing Supplies: You can order PUL fabric and other supplies here. I really like the site for PUL because it offers several size options. Jo-Ann Fabric and Craft and Hobby Lobby both sell a small line of PUL, but they don't have a huge selection. If you do purchase at those stores, make sure you use a coupon!

Easy Supply List for this eBook: This is a blog post I wrote with a list of supplies for this eBook.

FluffLove University has extensive information on cloth diapering.

KamSnaps: This is where I purchased my snap pliers and snaps. The prices are reasonable and the pliers can endure heavy use. If I were sewing a lot of cloth diapers or other items that required a bigger snap, I would definitely consider purchasing a snap press.

I hope you enjoyed this book. Please consider leaving a review with a few kind words.

[Click here to leave an Amazon review.](#)